PRESIDENTIAL
VISITS
BY
STATE

PRESIDENTIAL
VISITS
BY
STATE

A Travel Guide to the Homes, Libraries,
Museums, Birthplaces, and Final Resting Places
of the Presidents

Susan Alba

DEDICATION

To all of my children and grandchildren:
Heidi, Chris, Sam, Jameson, and Tristan
Joe, Amy, Josh, Andy, and Lucy
Jessica and Cristiano
Jodie, Jay, Madeline, and Violet
Dave, Cassie, and Rosalina

Always and forever, my biggest thank you is to my Guy,
my always positive and loving husband,
who is always on my side.

CONTENTS

ACKNOWLEDGMENTS

I wish a very heartfelt thank you to those who accompanied me to any of these presidential sites. Thank you, Madeline, Jessica, Heidi, Robin, Jodie and Jay, Andy and Polly, Dan and Diane, Kathy and Tom, and especially my husband, Guy.

Thank you to Allen, Kendra, Chrissy W., Elizabeth R., and Kennedy S. from Write My Wrongs for their superb editing, creative contributions, and attention to detail that no other editor could ever match.

I must express gratitude to Louis L. Picone, author and historian, who has written several informative books on presidential history. I recommend his works for an in-depth look at many of the locations listed in this book.

Also, a special thanks to Phlash Phelps phrom SiriusXM's '60s on 6 phor his interesting, inphormative, phun travel stories, and phor helping me phind some oph these hidden treasures in our phabulous country.

IT ALL STARTED WITH A SCRAPBOOK

I do not consider myself a historian; although I love to read and learn about American history, I consider it a hobby. My first presidential visit was during my senior year of high school when we had a class trip to Mount Vernon, Virginia. Years later, when my children were young, I enjoyed taking them to places like Plymouth Rock, Plimoth Plantation, and Old Sturbridge Village, where actors recreated life as it had been in early America.

When my children grew up, I became a teacher, and my love for history was ignited. I found that the fifth graders needed to have a fun way to learn about the United States. So, we did projects and presentations on states and presidents. We also spent countless hours learning about the past of our own state, Rhode Island.

Years later, on a trip to Virginia, I returned to Mount Vernon with my husband. This time, I appreciated the history so much more. We traveled to several historic presidential sites—I took so many pictures, and I needed to get them organized.

It all started with a scrapbook!

One weekend in Charlottesville, Virginia, my friend Polly and I went to Jefferson's Monticello. Polly suggested I print the photos I took that day and start a new scrapbook. I loved it! It gave me the idea to fill that binder with pages for every president and was the beginning of my quest to visit all of the presidential homes.

Although I have not visited all of the sites I reference, I wrote this book so that I would have a guide handy when I'm traveling. When I visit a state, I want to know about other nearby sites, so I began researching, buying books in the gift shops, and talking with other authors, guides, and visitors. I met so many people who also get excited when they visit a cemetery. I toured more sites, and my list just grew and grew, so I began to compile and organize pages of locations by state. People I spoke to asked me to publish it so they, too, could have the list. That's how this book came to be. Now that I'm organized, I can pick a state, continue my travels, and step into presidential history.

The first section of this book is listed alphabetically by state with a short description and the location of each presidential historical site. I have included the birthplaces, childhood homes, family homes, Summer White Houses, Winter White Houses, ancestral homes, retirement homes, presidential libraries and museums, and the final resting places of each president. For your convenience, I have also included websites for the National Park Service and National Archives and Records Administration, which will display locations and visiting hours (always check ahead; the hours do change). I did not include the history of each residence or the area surrounding it. I have, however, referenced several of my favorite presidential books by exceptional authors, who include in-depth researched histories of these sites.

In the second section, I've included a checklist of the presidents listed chronologically and the addresses of their historical sites. There, you can check off each visit you make to their birthplaces, childhood homes, family homes, Summer and Winter White Houses, museums and libraries, retirement homes, and final resting places.

I invite you to write in it, mark it up, and scribble notes and dates in your book as you travel. Contact me with other places you've found too! I hope you enjoy traveling to these sites as much as I have. Mostly, I hope you find my guide helpful. Happy travels, my friend!

ARKANSAS

1. **Fayetteville, Arkansas**
   Family Home: William and Hillary Clinton

2. **Hope, Arkansas**
   Birthplace: William Clinton
   Early Childhood Home: William Clinton
   Childhood Home: William Clinton
   Visitor Center and Museum: William Clinton

3. **Hot Springs, Arkansas**
   Boyhood Home: William Clinton
   Hot Springs High School: William Clinton

4. **Little Rock, Arkansas**
   Presidential Library and Museum: William Clinton

Fayetteville, Arkansas

William and Hillary Clinton
Family Home
Open to the public
Clinton House Museum[1]
930 West Clinton Drive
Fayetteville, Arkansas 72701

Open to the public year-round on Mondays, Tuesdays, Thursdays, Fridays, and Saturdays from 10:00 a.m. to 5:00 p.m. and on Sundays from 1:00 p.m. to 5:00 p.m. Closed on Wednesdays as well as on Thanksgiving, Christmas, and New Year's Day.

Bill Clinton moved to Fayetteville in 1973 to teach at the University of Arkansas School of Law. He bought this English-style bungalow, where he and Hillary married on October 11, 1975. The home, built in 1931, is where Bill and Hillary began their life together; they lived here until entering politics in 1978. The museum showcases memorabilia, photos, documents, and videos. See a replica of Hillary's wedding dress and stroll through her garden. Visit the gift shop and pick up a driving-tour map of other important Clinton sites.

---

[1] http://www.clintonhousemuseum.org

Hope, Arkansas

William Clinton
Birthplace
Not open to the public
Brazzel-Oakcrest Funeral Home (Formerly Julia Chester Hospital)
1001 South Main Street
Hope, Arkansas 71801

Bill Clinton was born William Jefferson Blythe III on August 19, 1946, at the Julia Chester Hospital. He is the son of Mrs. Virginia Blythe and was named after his late father, who had died three months earlier in a tragic car accident. The hospital Clinton was born in no longer exists; this location is now the site of a funeral home. There is a historical stone marker at the base of the home's flagpole.

Hope, Arkansas

William Clinton
Early Childhood Home
Open to the public
Clinton Center and Birthplace[2]
National Park Service
117 South Hervey Street
Hope, Arkansas 71801

Admission is free, and the home is open Mondays through Saturdays from 8:30 a.m. to 4:30 p.m. Closed on Thanksgiving, Christmas, and New Year's Day.

Clinton lived in his childhood home for the first four years of his life with his mother and grandparents. There are two stories, with a living room, kitchen, and dining room downstairs, and three bedrooms upstairs. Although built in 1917, the house has been restored to a 1950s style to reflect how Clinton's mother might remember it. The site includes a memorial to the president's mother: the Virginia Cassidy Blythe Clinton Kelley Memorial Garden.

---

[2] http://www.clintonchildhoodhomemuseum.com

Hope, Arkansas

William Clinton
Hope Visitor Center and Museum[3]
Open to the public
100 East Division Street
Hope, Arkansas 71801

Admission to the Hope Visitor Center and Museum is free, and it's open daily from 8:30 a.m. to 4:30 p.m. Closed on Thanksgiving, Christmas, and New Year's Day.

The Hope Visitor Center's depot has artifacts and photos of Clinton's 1992 campaign. Guests are invited to view an informative short film and talk to the very friendly staff about Clinton's early life.

---

[3] https://www.arkansas.com/hope/attractions-culture/hope-visitor-center-museum

Hope, Arkansas

William Clinton
Childhood Home
Not open to the public
321 East 13th Street
Hope, Arkansas 71801

When Bill's mother married Roger Clinton in 1950, the family moved into this small home. Billy adored his new little half-brother, Roger Jr., who was born in 1956. Bill changed his name to Clinton so everyone would know he and Roger were brothers. The house is now empty and is not open to visitors.

Hot Springs, Arkansas

William Clinton
Boyhood Home
Not open to the public
1011 Park Avenue
Hot Springs, Arkansas 71901

The Clintons relocated to this house when Bill was eight years old. The family lived there until 1961 and then moved to 213 Scully Street. He attended Hot Springs High School on 125 Oak Street, where he graduated in 1964. Clinton's high school building has been repurposed into an art gallery and housing complex, with a plaque at the front entrance noting Clinton's connection.

While you're in town, be sure to tour the Hot Springs National Park Visitor Center in the historic district on Central Avenue. You can visit the original bathhouses and see the bubbling hot springs.

Little Rock, Arkansas

William Clinton
Presidential Library and Museum
Open to the public
William J. Clinton Presidential Center and Park[4]
Administered by the National Archives and Records Administration
1200 President Clinton Avenue
Little Rock, Arkansas 72201

Open Mondays through Saturdays from 9:00 a.m. to 5:00 p.m. and on Sundays from 1:00 p.m. to 5:00 p.m. Closed on Thanksgiving, Christmas, and New Year's Day.

The Presidential Library is on the banks of the Arkansas River in Little Rock. Visit exhibits dedicated to Clinton's life as a child as well as before, during, and after his presidency. On display, you'll see his presidential limousine, a replica of the Cabinet Room, a timeline of his life, and many presidential gifts. The permanent exhibits give a glimpse into the inner workings of his White House years and the lives of the First Family. There are also changing temporary exhibitions on three floors of the library.

Dine at 42 Bar and Table, the Clinton Presidential Center's award-winning restaurant, for a delicious meal featuring locally grown ingredients. The restaurant is open for lunch from 11:00 a.m. to 2:00 p.m. every day of the week. Dinner is from 4:00 p.m. to 8:00 p.m. on Tuesdays and Wednesdays and from 4:00 p.m. to 9:00 p.m. on Thursdays through Saturdays. There is no dinner service on Sunday or Monday.

[4] https://www.clintonlibrary.gov/

CALIFORNIA

1. **Santa Barbara, California**
   Western White House: Ronald Reagan

2. **Simi Valley, California**
   Final Resting Place: Ronald Reagan
   Presidential Library and Museum: Ronald Reagan

3. **Yorba Linda, California**
   Birthplace: Richard Nixon
   Presidential Library and Museum: Richard Nixon
   Final Resting Place: Richard Nixon

Santa Barbara, California

Ronald Reagan
Western White House
Open to the public
Reagan Ranch Center Exhibit Galleries[5]
217 State Street
Santa Barbara, California 93101

Located on the historic Rancho Del Cielo (which itself is not open to the public), the Reagan Ranch Center Exhibit Gallery is open Mondays through Thursdays from 11:00 a.m. to 4:00 p.m. It is closed on holidays.

The Reagan Center in downtown Santa Barbara has videos of Reagan's speeches that offer a glimpse into his private life and time as president. There is a piece of the Berlin Wall, Reagan's blue Jeep, and a timetable of his life on display.

Thirty miles away, Rancho Del Cielo, the adobe-structure ranch home where Reagan lived for twenty-five years, is used by the Young America's Foundation for educational purposes. They allow students and supporters alike to visit and learn from the ranch.

---

[5] http://reaganranch.yaf.org/

Simi Valley, California

Ronald Reagan
Presidential Library and Museum
Open to the public
Ronald Reagan Presidential Library and Museum[6]
Administered by the National Archives and Records Administration
40 Presidential Drive
Simi Valley, California 93065

---

[6] https://www.reaganfoundation.org

Open on weekdays from 10:00 a.m. to 5:00 p.m. and on Saturdays and Sundays from 9:30 a.m. until 6:00 p.m.

The museum's one-hundred-acre site is one of California's most beautiful tourist attractions. Glimpse fragments of the Berlin Wall, torn down under Reagan's bold leadership during the Cold War, and view an exact replica of the Oval Office decorated with Western art as it appeared during the Reagan presidency. Follow the life of Reagan from his childhood, on through his acting career, and to his presidency of the United States. There are historical displays, photos, documents, family memorabilia, and videos of Reagan's life. Visit the amazing three-story, 90,000-square-foot Air Force One Pavilion, and climb aboard "the flying White House."

Stop for lunch at the Ronald Reagan Pub or Reagan's Country Café, and tour the beautifully manicured grounds and gardens leading to Reagan's final resting place.

Simi Valley, California

Ronald Reagan
Final Resting Place
Open to the public
Ronald Reagan Presidential Library and Museum[7]
Administered by the National Archives and Records Administration
40 Presidential Drive
Simi Valley, California 93065

Ronald Reagan died on June 5, 2004. He was buried on a hillside with spectacular views of the Simi Valley Mountains. Ronald and Nancy Reagan are entombed in the underground crypt on the grounds of the Presidential Library.

---

[7] https://www.reaganfoundation.org

Yorba Linda, California

Richard Nixon
Birthplace, Final Resting Place, Presidential Library and Museum
Open to the public
Richard Nixon Presidential Library and Museum[8]
18001 Yorba Linda Boulevard
Yorba Linda, California 92886

Open on Mondays through Saturdays from 10:00 a.m. to 5:00 p.m. and on Sundays from 11:00 a.m. to 5:00 p.m. There are three historical markers here.

The home where Richard Nixon was born on January 9, 1913, is registered as a U.S. National Historic Landmark. The house was a mail-order kit built by Nixon's father. The bungalow-style home had no electricity and no toilet when built. You can tour the humble farmhouse with its original furniture as it was in the 1910s and see the bed in which Richard Nixon was born. This home can be viewed as part of the museum tour, which is offered during visitor hours.

At this museum, you can learn about the president from his early years to his funeral and burial. See the limousine used by Nixon, the same one used by Presidents Johnson, Ford, and Carter. Climb aboard Marine One, the presidential helicopter flown when Nixon left office, and view a replica of the East Room of the White House. Listen to recordings of the "White House Tapes." Enjoy the nine-acre grounds while spending time in the First Lady's gardens.

Richard Nixon died on April 22, 1994, and was buried next to his wife, Pat, just a few steps away from his birthplace. The final resting place of Richard and Pat Nixon is on the grounds of the Richard Nixon Presidential Library and Museum. Each grave is marked with a small black granite stone.

---

[8] https://www.nixonfoundation.org

CANADA

Both the Canadian government and the United States government jointly administer Campobello International Park.

1. **New Brunswick, Canada**
   Summer Home: Franklin Delano Roosevelt
   Passport Required

New Brunswick, Canada

Franklin D. Roosevelt
Summer Home
Open to the public; passport required
Roosevelt Campobello International Park[9]
National Park Service
459 Route 774
Welshpool, New Brunswick E5E 1A4, Canada

---

[9] https://www.nps.gov/roca/index.htm

Open seven days a week from the Saturday following Victoria Day (the Saturday prior to U.S. Memorial Day) through Canadian Thanksgiving (U.S. Columbus Day) from 10:00 a.m. to 6:00 p.m. ADT (9:00 a.m. to 5:00 p.m. EDT).

Explore Franklin and Eleanor's summer home on this beautiful island. The memorabilia-filled thirty-four-room cottage, with eighteen bedrooms, was the Roosevelt family's summer home for over fifty-six years.

President Lyndon B. Johnson and Prime Minister Lester Pearson created the Roosevelt Campobello International Park in 1964. Both the Canadian government and the United States government jointly administer the park as a memorial to President Roosevelt. Over the bridge, just across the international border off of Maine's northernmost coast, is Campobello Island, New Brunswick, Canada (a passport is required).

Plan to spend time at the visitor center, where you can view a short film, then take self-guided tours of the Roosevelt Cottage and the Hubbard Cottage. Park rangers are available at both buildings to answer any questions. Walk through the flower gardens, and take in the scenic views of the Atlantic Ocean.

While on the island, enjoy walking and biking the many trails on the 2,800-acre park overlooking the ocean. Have "Tea with Eleanor" at the Hubbard Cottage to hear stories about Eleanor Roosevelt. Tickets for this event can be purchased from the visitor center.

CONNECTICUT

1. **New Haven, Connecticut**
   Birthplace: George W. Bush
   Childhood Home: George W. Bush

New Haven, Connecticut

George W. Bush
Birthplace
Not open to the public
Yale New Haven Hospital
20 York Street
New Haven, Connecticut 06511

George W. Bush was born on July 6, 1946, at Yale New Haven Hospital, then called Grace-New Haven Community Hospital, while his father was a student at Yale.

New Haven, Connecticut

George W. Bush
Childhood Home
Not open to the public
37 Hillhouse Avenue
New Haven, Connecticut 06511

As a newborn, George W. Bush lived in a one-family home that had been converted into apartments for veterans and their families. The homestead is now used by the Yale Economics Department.

DELAWARE

1. **Rehoboth Beach, Delaware**
   Summer Home: Joseph Biden

2. **Wilmington, Delaware**
   Family Home: Joseph Biden

Rehoboth Beach, Delaware

Joseph Biden
Summer Home
Not open to the public
Rehoboth Beach, Delaware 19971

Joseph Biden and his wife, Jill, purchased this home in 2017 for $2.7 million. The house is close to the beach and overlooks the Cape Henlopen State Park. It is a private residence and not open to the public for tours.

Wilmington, Delaware

Joseph Biden
Family Home
Not open to the public
1209 Barley Mill Road
Wilmington, Delaware 19807

Joe Biden built this 6,850-square-foot home on the four acres of lakefront property he bought in the Greenville suburb of Wilmington. It is the family's main residence. The home is valued at $2 million.

ENGLAND

1. **United Kingdom, England**
   Ancestral Home: George Washington

United Kingdom

George Washington
Ancestral Home
Open to the public
Sulgrave Manor[10]
Manor Road
Sulgrave, Banbury OX17 2SD
United Kingdom

Open to the public spring through fall and also in the winter for special events and school tours.

This Tudor-style home was built in the mid-1500s by Lawrence Washington, George Washington's five-times-great-grandfather, and has been restored to the time period of Washington's ancestors with furniture and displays in the bedrooms, parlor, and the Great Hall. The house was presented to the people of Britain and the U.S. as a memorial to George Washington.

Costumed actors teach visitors about the Washington family and the events that led them to seek a new life. Stroll through the gardens and visit the Buttery Café while you're there.

---

[10] http://www.sulgravemanor.org.uk/

FLORIDA

1. **Key West, Florida**
   Little White House: Harry S. Truman
   Historical Park: Zachary Taylor

2. **Palm Beach, Florida**
   Winter White House: John F. Kennedy
   Winter White House: Donald Trump

Key West, Florida

Harry S. Truman
Little White House
Open to the public
Harry S. Truman Little White House[11]
111 Front Street
Key West, Florida 33040

Open daily from 9:00 a.m. to 4:30 p.m.

The Harry S. Truman Little White House was originally built in 1890 by the U.S. Navy and served as the command headquarters during the Spanish-American War, World War I, and World War II. In 1946, the historic building began serving as the Winter White House. In 1991, the home opened to the public as Florida's only presidential historical museum. Tour the home to see rooms with mostly original furnishings, take a self-guided tour of the botanical gardens, and visit the gift shop.

---

[11] http://www.trumanlittlewhitehouse.com/

Key West, Florida

Zachary Taylor
Historical Park
Open to the public
Fort Zachary Taylor Historic State Park[12]
601 Howard England Way
Key West, Florida 33040

The park is open year-round from 8:00 a.m. until sundown, while the fort closes at 5:00 p.m.

Upon completion of the fort in 1850, Zachary Taylor suddenly died while in office at the White House, and the fort was then named after him. Fort Zachary Taylor played important roles in the Civil War and the Spanish-American War. Visitors can enjoy bicycling, walking a short nature trail within the park, and exploring the largest surviving collection of Civil War artillery belonging to the park. Guided tours are available daily. The park's concessionaire offers an expanded menu with beachfront dining and a gift shop.

---

[12] https://www.floridastateparks.org/park/Fort-Taylor

Palm Beach, Florida

John F. Kennedy
Winter White House
Not open to the public
Kennedy Family Home
1095 North Ocean Boulevard
Palm Beach, Florida 33480

Joseph and Rose Kennedy purchased this home in 1933 for $120,000. It is where they spent the winters with their son, the future president John F. Kennedy, and his siblings. Later, as president, Kennedy and his family used the estate as his Winter White House. After sixty-two years in the Kennedy family, the house was sold in 1995 for $31 million. Much of the original furnishings were sold at public auction.

Palm Beach, Florida

Donald Trump
Winter White House
Not open to the public
Mar-a-Lago
1100 South Ocean Boulevard
Palm Beach, Florida 33415

Donald Trump bought this twenty-acre estate for $10 million and turned it into a private club. The home was built in the 1920s. There are 126 rooms in the mansion, with 58 bedrooms and 33 bathrooms. The home is private and is not open to the public. It is now valued at $160 million.

GEORGIA

1. **Atlanta, Georgia**
   Presidential Library and Museum: Jimmy Carter

2. **Augusta, Georgia**
   Childhood Home: Thomas Woodrow Wilson

3. **Plains, Georgia**
   Childhood Home: Jimmy Carter
   Birthplace: Jimmy Carter

4. **Warm Springs, Georgia**
   Little White House: Franklin Delano Roosevelt

Atlanta, Georgia

Jimmy Carter
Presidential Library and Museum
Open to the public
Jimmy Carter Presidential Library and Museum[13]
Administered by the National Archives and Records Administration
441 John Lewis Freedom Parkway NE
Atlanta, Georgia 30307

Open on Mondays through Saturdays from 9:00 a.m. to 4:45 p.m. and on Sundays from noon to 4:45 p.m. Closed on Thanksgiving, Christmas, and New Year's Day.

There are valuable documents, records, and letters on display here. See campaign memorabilia and gifts given to the First Family. View photos, films, and speeches, as well as a replica of the Oval Office. There is also a nicely done display with a kiosk dedicated to each of the thirteen National Archive Presidential Libraries with photos, locations, and their significance. There is a research center with many documents, videos, and photos, as well as Carter's 2002 Nobel Peace Prize on display at the museum. The gift shop has books and memorabilia related to Carter's life and career. Be sure to stop at the Little Café for a light lunch, where you can sit outside on the stone patio and enjoy your meal while overlooking the beautifully manicured grounds and pond.

---

[13] https://www.jimmycarterlibrary.gov/

Augusta, Georgia

Thomas Woodrow Wilson
Childhood Home
Open to the public
Woodrow Wilson Boyhood Home[14]
419 Seventh Street
Augusta, Georgia 30901

Tours are offered Thursdays through Saturdays on the hour from 10:00 a.m. to 4:00 p.m. Closed on Thanksgiving and Christmas.

Built in 1859, the Wilson Manse shows life as it was for "Tommy" growing up during the Civil War and Reconstruction. Thomas Woodrow Wilson lived here from 1860 to 1870 while his father was serving as minister.

Tour the home and walk through the gardens. The house has been restored to look as it did during the 1860s and is owned and operated by Historic Augusta, Inc. The gardens have a showcase of plants that were there during the time the Wilson family lived on the property.

---

[14] http://www.wilsonboyhoodhome.org/

Plains, Georgia

Jimmy Carter
Childhood Home
Open to the public
Jimmy Carter National Historic Site[15]
National Park Service
300 North Bond Street
Plains, Georgia 31780

This historic site is open daily except on Thanksgiving, Christmas, and New Year's Day. The Plains High School Visitor Center and Museum is open from 9:00 a.m. to 5:00 p.m. The Train Depot Museum is open from 9:00 a.m. to 4:30 p.m. The Jimmy Carter Boyhood Home is open from 10:00 a.m. to 5:00 p.m. Walking tours of the farm are conducted on Saturdays and Sundays at 11:30 a.m. and 3:30 p.m. The Carter Private Residence and Compound is not open to the public.

The Carter family moved into this house in 1928, where they grew cotton, peanuts, fruits, and vegetables. Carter lived here until 1941, when he went away to college. The house opened to the public in 1996. The park consists of three parts: Start at the visitor center, housed in the former Plains High School, where Jimmy and his wife Rosalynn attended. Here, you'll find a classroom furnished as it was in the 1930s, the principal's office, and the auditorium. Next, visit the Plains Depot, where Carter had his 1976 campaign headquarters. Finally, visit the Jimmy Carter Boyhood Home. The house has been restored to the way it was when they moved here in 1928, without electricity or plumbing. Visitors can pick up a self-guided-tour brochure to explore the entire park and walking paths. Audio is available through a narrated cell-phone tour or by pushing buttons both inside and outside of buildings.

---

[15] https://www.nps.gov/nr/travel/presidents/jimmy_carter_nhs.html

Plains, Georgia

Jimmy Carter
Birthplace
Not open to the public
Lillian G. Carter Health and Rehabilitation Nursing Center
225 Hospital Street
Plains, Georgia 31780

Formerly known as Wise Sanitarium, the hospital Carter was born in is now the Lillian G. Carter Nursing Center. A marker indicates that "Jimmy Carter, son of Earl and Lillian Carter, was born here on October 1, 1924. He was the first president of the United States to be born in a hospital. On January 21, 1936, a fire damaged the building."

Warm Springs, Georgia

Franklin Delano Roosevelt
Little White House
Open to the public
Little White House Historic Site[16]
401 Little White House Road
Warm Springs, Georgia 31830

Open daily from 9:00 a.m. to 4:45 p.m. Closed on Thanksgiving, Christmas, and New Year's Day.

FDR built this modest six-room cottage in 1932 before becoming president. He moved here hoping that the healing waters of the warm springs would be a cure for his polio. He swam in the springs and received therapy, and although it did bring him some relief, it did not cure his illness.

Tour the house and see it much as it was left when he died here on April 12, 1945, of a cerebral hemorrhage. Walk the grounds of the Memorial Fountain and the Walk of the States. In the small museum, you can see the two classic cars and the 1938 Ford that belonged to FDR and view a film in the auditorium. See the unfinished portrait that was being painted when he passed away. Also, stop at the nearby pools to feel the warm mineral spring water.

---

[16] http://gastateparks.org/LittleWhiteHouse/

HAWAII

1. **Honolulu, Hawaii**
   Birthplace: Barack Obama
   Childhood Home: Barack Obama

Honolulu, Hawaii

Barack Obama
Birthplace
Not open to the public
Kapiʻolani Medical Center for Women and Children
1319 Punahou Street
Honolulu, Hawaii 96826

Barack Hussein Obama II was born on August 4, 1961, at The Kapiʻolani Medical Center for Women and Children. It is still an operating hospital; it does not have a plaque or monument to recognize Obama's birthplace.

Honolulu, Hawaii

Barack Obama
Childhood Home
Not open to the public
6085 Kalaniana'ole Highway
Honolulu, Hawaii 96821

Barack Obama spent most of his childhood in Hawaii. His first home is a private residence and is not open to the public. There is no marker or monument.

ILLINOIS

1. **Chicago, Illinois**
   Family Home: Barack Obama
   Presidential Library and Museum: Barack Obama

2. **Dixon, Illinois**
   Childhood Home: Ronald Reagan

3. **Eureka, Illinois**
   Presidential Museum: Ronald Reagan

4. **Galena, Illinois**
   Family Home: Ulysses S. Grant

5. **Lincoln, Illinois**
   Museum: Abraham Lincoln

6. **Petersburg, Illinois**
   Family Home: Abraham Lincoln

7. **Springfield, Illinois**
   Family Home: Abraham Lincoln
   Presidential Museum: Abraham Lincoln
   Presidential Library: Abraham Lincoln
   Final Resting Place: Abraham Lincoln

8. **Tampico, Illinois**
Birthplace: Ronald Reagan
Childhood Home: Ronald Reagan

Chicago, Illinois

Barack Obama
Family Home
Not open to the public
Barack Obama Family Home
5046 South Greenwood Avenue
Chicago, Illinois 60615

Although the Obamas currently reside in a rented house in Washington D.C., they still call Chicago home. Their beautiful Georgian-Revival mansion is part of the Chicago neighborhood tours. It is in a residential area that is great for strolling. There are six bedrooms and six bathrooms. Obama bought the home in 2005 for $1.65 million.

Chicago, Illinois

Barack Obama
Presidential Library and Museum
Currently under construction. Opening date unknown
Barack Obama Center[17]
Jackson Park
Chicago, Illinois 60615

Barack Obama's Presidential Library and Museum is currently under construction, and the opening date is yet unknown. Upon completion, it will showcase collections of documents, books, clothing, furnishings, and other artifacts that represent the Obama administration. It will be the first fully digital presidential library.

---

[17] https://www.obamalibrary.gov/

Dixon, Illinois

Ronald Reagan
Childhood Home
Open to the public
Ronald Reagan Boyhood Home and Visitors Center[18]
816 South Hennepin Avenue
Dixon, Illinois 61021

Open Tuesdays through Saturdays from 10:00 a.m. to 4:00 p.m., April 1 to October 30.

The Reagan family moved to this Queen-Anne-style home in 1920 when Reagan was ten years old. He lived here until he graduated from college at twenty-two years old. The home has been restored with furnishings of the time period. The docents tell stories of the family and the house. Tour the house, visitor center, and gift shop.

---

[18] http://reaganhome.org/

Eureka, Illinois

Ronald Reagan
Presidential Museum
Open to the public
Ronald Reagan Museum[19]
300 East College Avenue
Eureka, Illinois 61530

Open on Mondays through Fridays from 8:00 a.m. to 5:00 p.m. during the school year and from 9:00 a.m. to 4:00 p.m. during the summer. Closed on Saturdays and Sundays.

Located on the campus of Eureka College, where Reagan graduated in 1932, there is a large collection of Reagan objects on display. See numerous accolades, including his Golden Globe Award. His robe and diploma are on display as well as letters written by Reagan and many more personal items. As you walk the campus, stop in the Reagan Peace Garden and at several other sites dedicated to Ronald Reagan.

---

[19] reagan.eureka.edu

Galena, Illinois

Ulysses S. Grant
Family Home
Open to the public
Grant Home[20]
500 Bouthillier Street
Galena, Illinois 61036

Open on Wednesdays through Sundays from 9:00 a.m. to 4:45 p.m. Closed on Mondays, Tuesdays, and holidays.

This Greek-Revival-style house that Grant rented until his presidency is open to the public. The brick home has been restored to how it looked when it was constructed in 1860. Stop at the Old Market House Welcome Center on Commerce Street for information on several parks and historic homes in Galena.

---

[20] http://www.granthome.com/

Susan Alba

Lincoln, Illinois

Abraham Lincoln
Museum
Open to the public
Lincoln Heritage Museum[21]
1115 Nicholson Road
Lincoln, Illinois 62656

Open Mondays through Fridays from 9:00 a.m. to 4:00 p.m. and on Saturdays from 1:00 p.m. to 4:00 p.m. Closed on Sundays and Lincoln College holidays and breaks.

Interactive exhibits put you into the shoes of Abraham Lincoln as you experience many periods of his life with audio and video presentations. See rare pieces relating to Lincoln and the Civil War: maps, photos, and timelines. View the Boarding House exhibit of Lincoln's death. Due to graphic imagery, some of the Civil War exhibits are not suitable for small children.

---

[21] http://museum.lincolncollege.edu/

Petersburg, Illinois

Abraham Lincoln
Young Adult Home
Open to the public
Lincoln's New Salem[22]
15588 History Lane
Petersburg, Illinois 62675

Open daily from 9:00 a.m. to 5:00 p.m.

Trace the footsteps of Abraham Lincoln in the village where he spent six years of his early adulthood. The village buildings have been historically reconstructed on their original foundations. Walk through seven hundred acres and visit twenty-three historically furnished log houses, stores, taverns, a school, a gristmill, and many other buildings as you hear stories about Lincoln. Interpreters dressed in period clothing reenact life in the 1800s, when Lincoln lived and worked here. View a film at the visitor center to learn about the president's life in New Salem, and visit the small museum. There's a concession stand and a picnic area to enjoy as well as a lovely gift shop with many books and memorabilia.

---

[22] http://lincolnsnewsalem.com

Springfield, Illinois

Abraham Lincoln
Family Home
Open to the public
Lincoln Home National Historic Site[23]
National Park Service
413 South Eighth Street
Springfield, Illinois 62701

Open daily from 8:30 a.m. to 5:00 p.m. except for Thanksgiving, Christmas, and New Year's Day.

Lincoln bought this house in 1844. The Lincoln Home was built in 1839 and has been restored to appear as it did in the 1860s, with much of the original furniture. Abraham and Mary Todd Lincoln lived in the twelve-room Greek-Revival home with their boys for seventeen years. This is known as "the only house that Lincoln ever owned." During the tour, hold the same handrail that Abraham Lincoln touched over one hundred years ago. Tickets for the tour are free but must be picked up at the visitor center, where you can view a film of Lincoln's life and visit the gift shop. Tour the kitchen, living room, dining room, and bedrooms inside the home as docents tell informative stories of Lincoln's time here. Enjoy exploring the surrounding neighborhood of twelve structures that have been renovated to how they looked when Lincoln walked these same streets.

---

[23] https://www.nps.gov/liho/index.htm

Springfield, Illinois

Abraham Lincoln
Presidential Library and Museum
Open to the public
Abraham Lincoln Presidential Library and Museum[24]
212 North Sixth Street
Springfield, Illinois 62701

The museum is open daily from 9:00 a.m. to 5:00 p.m., and the library is open Monday through Friday from 9:00 a.m. to 5:00 p.m.

Explore exhibits ranging from a replica of Lincoln's birth in a log cabin to his presidency. Many historical articles are publicly shown in the museum, and there are displays with artifacts like clothing, jewelry, and letters. View several films about Lincoln's life. There are also changing exhibits and presentations. The separate library is for the study and safekeeping of historical artifacts. A large gift shop has an extensive selection of Lincoln books and memorabilia.

---

[24] https://presidentlincoln.illinois.gov/

Springfield, Illinois

Abraham Lincoln
Final Resting Place
Open to the public
Oak Ridge Cemetery[25]
1441 Monument Avenue
Springfield, Illinois 62702

The cemetery is open daily from 7:00 a.m. to 8:00 p.m., and the tomb is open for tours Monday through Friday from 8:00 a.m. to 4:30 p.m. Oak Ridge Cemetery is the largest cemetery in Illinois and is the second-most visited cemetery in the United States after Arlington National Cemetery.

"Now he belongs to the ages." These were the words of Secretary of War Edwin Stanton when Abraham Lincoln died on April 15, 1865. Lincoln's body was brought to the White House, where he was embalmed and prepared for the long journey from Washington D.C. to his final resting place in Springfield, Illinois. During his twenty days of travel, there were thousands of mourners, Black and White people together, paying their respects to the president. He was finally buried in the Lincoln Vault with his son Willie, who had died in the White House at age eleven. This vault is part of the tour at Oak Ridge Cemetery.

Lincoln was moved several times before arriving at this final resting place in 1901. The tomb was completed in 1874 and stands 117 feet tall. Lincoln's wife, Mary Todd Lincoln, and three of their sons, Edward, William, and Thomas, are also buried in the tomb.

Tampico, Illinois

Ronald Reagan
Birthplace
Open to the public
Ronald Reagan Birthplace and Museum[26]
111 South Main Street
Tampico, Illinois 61283

Reagan's birthplace is open April through October and on weekends in March. The museum is open Mondays through Saturdays from 10:00 a.m. to 4:00 p.m. and on Sundays from 1:00 p.m. to 4:00 p.m. Closed on Easter and Mother's Day. Closed in November, December, and January.

President Ronald Reagan was born on February 6, 1911, in an apartment above a bakery. The building was constructed in 1895, and in 1919, the bakery was purchased by First National Bank, which continued inhabiting it until the 1930s. The apartment where Reagan was born is now restored to look as it did in 1911. The bank has also been refinished as a museum and looks like a working establishment. A store south of the bank is now the gift shop of the Ronald Reagan Birthplace and Museum.

---

[26] http://www.tampicohistoricalsociety.com/R_Reagan_Birthplace_Museum.html

Tampico, Illinois

Ronald Reagan
Childhood Home
Not open to the public
104 Glassburn Street[27]
Tampico, Illinois 61283

Shortly after the birth of Ronald Reagan, the family moved into a larger two-story home in the same town, now across the street from Reagan Park. They did not live in this home for very long. It is currently a private residence and is not open to the public.

INDIANA

1. **Indianapolis, Indiana**
   Family Home: Benjamin Harrison
   Final Resting Place: Benjamin Harrison

2. **Lincoln City, Indiana**
   Childhood Home: Abraham Lincoln

3. **Vincennes, Indiana**
   Family Home: William Henry Harrison

Indianapolis, Indiana

Benjamin Harrison
Family Home
Open to the public
Benjamin Harrison House[28]
1230 North Delaware Street
Indianapolis, Indiana 46202

Open Mondays through Saturdays from 10:00 a.m. to 3:30 p.m. and on Sundays in June and July from 12:30 p.m. to 3:30 p.m.

This home was constructed in 1875 for Benjamin Harrison and his first wife, Caroline. The Harrison Home is elegantly furnished with Victorian-era pieces, 80 percent of which belonged to the Harrison family. Their presidential china is displayed in the formal dining room. The wallpaper and chandeliers are original, and many personal possessions are on display. Purchase tickets for the tour from the gift shop located in the barn. There are many items in the gift shop, including a reproduction of the presidential china.

---

[28] http://bhpsite.org/

Indianapolis, Indiana

Benjamin Harrison
Final Resting Place
Open to the public
Crown Hill Funeral Home and Cemetery[29]
700 West 38th Street
Indianapolis, Indiana 46208

Benjamin Harrison died on March 13, 1901. He is buried in a location that he chose: section thirty-one, lot fifty-seven. The grave is marked with a ten-foot-tall tomb made of Vermont granite. The cemetery is in the National Register of Historic Places, and there is a historic marker and American flag at the site.

---

[29] http://www.crownhill.org/index.html

Lincoln City, Indiana

Abraham Lincoln
Boyhood Home
Open to the public
Lincoln Boyhood National Memorial
National Park Service
3027 East South Street
Lincoln City, Indiana 47552

Open daily from 8:00 a.m. to 5:00 p.m. from April through September and 8:00 a.m. to 3:00 p.m. from October through March. Closed Thanksgiving, Christmas, and New Year's Day.

Begin your tour at the National Visitor Center to view a fifteen-minute video explaining life as it was for Abraham Lincoln as a young boy on the farm. Visit the log cabin and outbuildings to see what life was like in the 1820s at the Living Historical Farm. Tour the gardens as workers in period-style clothing tend to the crops.

The park museum contains exhibits and artifacts of the life of the Lincoln family. Explore the grounds to visit the grave of Nancy Hanks Lincoln, Abraham Lincoln's mother, who died here in 1818 when Abe was nine years old.

Vincennes, Indiana

William Henry Harrison
Family Home
Open to the public
Grouseland, Harrison Mansion, "White House of the West"[30]
3 West Scott Street
Vincennes, Indiana 47591

Open Mondays through Saturdays from 10:00 a.m. to 5:00 p.m. and on Sundays from 12:00 p.m. to 5:00 p.m. from March through December. Reduced hours during January and February. Closed on Easter, Thanksgiving, Christmas, and New Year's Day; closed on Mondays in January and February.

William Henry Harrison built the Harrison Mansion in 1804. It was constructed on the banks of the Wabash River using handmade bricks, designed as a fortress with walls over a foot thick, and could've been used as a refuge during times of hostility. The house is restored to the time when Harrison lived here, with many period pieces and several original furnishings. On display are many artifacts from the presidential campaign known as "Tippecanoe and Tyler Too." The home is named Grouseland for the game birds in the area. The friendly, knowledgeable staff welcome visitors and are happy to answer questions about the presidential home and the history of the area. There is also a historic marker in front of the house.

---

[30] http://www.grouseland.org

IOWA

1. **West Branch, Iowa**
   Birthplace: Herbert Hoover
   Presidential Library and Museum: Herbert Hoover
   Final Resting Place: Herbert Hoover

West Branch, Iowa

Herbert Hoover
Birthplace
Open to the public
Herbert Hoover National Historic Site[31]
National Park Service
110 Parkside Drive
West Branch, Iowa 52358

Open daily from 9:00 a.m. to 5:00 p.m. Closed on Thanksgiving, Christmas, and New Year's Day.

Herbert Hoover was born on August 10, 1874, in a tiny cottage built by his father and grandfather in 1871. The fourteen-by-twenty-foot cottage has only two rooms; one serves as the kitchen, parlor, and dining area, and the other is the bedroom. Hoover lived here until 1879, when the family moved to a larger house. The home had many owners in the following years until 1935, when Allan Hoover, Herbert's son, purchased the property and returned it to his father. The cottage was restored, and on August 10, 1972, the home was opened to the public. The birthplace is part of the Herbert Hoover Historic Site.

---

[31] https://www.nps.gov/heho/index.htm

West Branch, Iowa

Herbert Hoover
Presidential Library and Museum
Open to the public
Herbert Hoover Presidential Library and Museum[32]
Administered by the National Archives and Records Administration
210 Parkside Drive
West Branch, Iowa 52358

Open daily from 9:00 a.m. to 5:00 p.m. Closed on Thanksgiving, Christmas, and New Year's Day.

At the library, there are millions of pages of documents, photos, and presidential materials. In the museum, visit the nine galleries that bring you through Hoover's life and his presidency. The Roaring Twenties, The Great Depression, and Humanitarian Years are just a few of the exhibits you can visit. There is a gift shop with books and memorabilia. At the Herbert Hoover National Historic Site, start at the visitor center, where you can view a film about Hoover's life in West Branch and get a map and guide for your self-guided tour. The historic site precinct in West Branch includes the cottage where Herbert Hoover was born, a blacksmith shop, the Quaker Meeting House, a schoolhouse, the Presidential Library and Museum, and the president's grave.

---

[32] https://hoover.archives.gov/

West Branch, Iowa

Herbert Hoover
Final Resting Place
Open to the public.
Herbert Hoover Presidential Library and Museum[33]
National Park Service
110 Parkside Drive
West Branch, Iowa 52358

Herbert Hoover died on October 20, 1964, at ninety years old. He is buried in West Branch, on the hill next to the cottage he was born in. The grave is marked with a simple headstone. His wife, Lou Henry Hoover, who predeceased Hoover, was reinterred next to her husband.

IRELAND

1. **Cullybackey, Antrim, Ireland**
   Ancestral Home: Chester A. Arthur

2. **Dungannon, United Kingdom**
   Ancestral Home: Ulysses S. Grant

3. **Wexford, Ireland**
   Ancestral Home: John F. Kennedy

Cullybackey, Antrim, Ireland

Chester A. Arthur
Ancestral Home
Open to the public
The Arthur Cottage[34]
21A Dreen Road
Cullybackey, Ballymena BT42 1EB,
County Antrim, Northern Ireland

The Arthur Cottage in the village of Cullybackey, County Antrim, Northern Ireland, is the ancestral home of Chester A. Arthur, the son of a Baptist preacher who emigrated to the United States. At the restored thatched cottage, see how the Arthur family lived in the late eighteenth century. Local ladies dress in period costumes and answer questions about Arthur's ancestors. There are baking demonstrations, and you can sample homemade Irish soda bread and pancakes. I found out about this home shortly after returning from Ireland, where I had been tracing my own ancestry. Now, I have a reason to return. I can't wait!

---

[34] http://www.discovernorthernireland.com/Arthur-Cottage-and-Interpretative-Centre-Cullybackey-Ballymena-P8218

Dungannon, United Kingdom

Ulysses S. Grant
Ancestral Home
Open to the public
U.S. Grant Ancestral Homestead
45 Dergenagh Road
Dungannon BT70 ITW
County Tyrone, Northern Ireland
United Kingdom

Open daily from 9:00 a.m. to 6:00 p.m.

The Simpson-Grant Ancestral Homestead is related to Grant through his mother's family line. The estate and farm have been restored to a mid-nineteenth-century style and appearance, with some original mud walls still exposed. John Simpson, the grandfather of U. S. Grant, lived here until he was twenty-two years old. View the picnic areas and the wildlife gardens on your self-guided visit.

Wexford, Ireland

John F. Kennedy
Ancestral Home
Open to the public
The Kennedy Homestead[35]
Dunganstown, New Ross,
County Wexford, Ireland

Open daily from 9:30 a.m. to 5:00 p.m. Closed on holidays.

Follow the Irish-American family through three generations, from the Irish famine to the presidency of the United States of America. The homestead, which is still being farmed today, is the birthplace of Kennedy's great-grandfather Patrick Kennedy. The museum is dedicated to "those who went away and those who stayed behind." Trace the story of the Kennedy family through an interpretive exhibit that explores the situations that led to the departure of Patrick Kennedy from Ireland in 1848. President Kennedy visited the homestead in 1963, where he later addressed the Irish president, saying, "I want to thank you for a visit that has been one of the most moving experiences of my life." The Kennedy Homestead is only an hour's drive from my own ancestral home that I found in Tipperary, Ireland.

[35] www.kennedyhomestead.ie

KANSAS

1. **Abilene, Kansas**
   Presidential Library and Museum: Dwight D. Eisenhower
   Childhood Home: Dwight D. Eisenhower
   Final Resting Place: Dwight D. Eisenhower

Abilene, Kansas

Dwight D. Eisenhower
Presidential Library and Museum
Open to the public
Eisenhower Presidential Library, Museum, and Boyhood Home[36]
Administered by the National Archives and Records Administration
200 Southeast Fourth Street
Abilene, Kansas 67410

Open August through May from 9:00 a.m. to 4:45 p.m. and in June and July from 8:00 a.m. to 5:45 p.m. Closed on Thanksgiving, Christmas, and New Year's Day.

The site of the Eisenhower Presidential Library, Museum, and Boyhood Home is a beautiful twenty-two-acre campus. Plan to spend several hours touring each exhibit. Buy your tour tickets in the visitor center, where you can also view a twenty-five-minute film. Then, exit to the campus and walk the beautifully manicured grounds. Tour the boyhood home with a knowledgeable docent; visit both the museum and the library, where you'll need plenty of time at the many interactive exhibits; and take a picture at the Ike statue that stands tall in the center of the grounds. Walk to the far end of the campus to the pylons, each with a beautiful dedication. And finally, visit his final resting place in the breathtaking Meditation Chapel. This is a spectacular campus dedicated to a great president. You'll want to return to the visitor center at the end of your trip to browse the gift shop. Here, you'll find many books and memorabilia dedicated to Dwight D. Eisenhower.

The Presidential Library is a research facility that contains historical records, papers, photographs, films, and artifacts. The second-floor gallery includes alternating exhibits from important events during Eisenhower's presidency. The newly renovated Presidential Museum is in a separate building across the beautiful campus, complete with all-new interactive exhibits where you can "Meet Ike and Mamie again...for the first time." The museum interprets the life

---

[36] https://www.eisenhowerlibrary.gov/

of Eisenhower from his birth, through his childhood, during his presidency, and until his death in 1969. There are also exhibits on the life of Mamie Eisenhower and the impact and importance of the First Lady. Watch videos and view photos, and see thousands of artifacts depicting the life of the president.

Abilene, Kansas

Dwight D. Eisenhower
Childhood Home
Open to the public
Eisenhower Presidential Library, Museum, & Boyhood Home
200 Southeast Fourth Street
Abilene, Kansas 67410

Open from 9:00 a.m. to 4:45 p.m. from August through May and from 8:00 a.m. to 5:45 p.m. during June and July. Closed on Thanksgiving, Christmas, and New Year's Day.

Explore Eisenhower's life, beginning in his boyhood home that the family moved to from Texas when their son Dwight was a year old. The house was built in 1887. As a boy, the future president worked here in the gardens and the creamery after school. The home has furnishings from the period during which the Eisenhower family lived here, from 1898 until Mrs. Eisenhower's death in 1946.

Abilene, Kansas

Dwight D. Eisenhower
Final Resting Place
Open to the public
The Meditation Chapel
Eisenhower Presidential Library, Museum, & Boyhood Home
200 Southeast Fourth Street
Abilene, Kansas 67410

The Meditation Chapel is located across from the Eisenhower Boyhood Home. The building was planned by Eisenhower and built before he died on March 28, 1969. Inside are three marble panels and plaques for Dwight D. Eisenhower, his wife Mamie Doud Eisenhower, and their firstborn son Doud Dwight Eisenhower. Colorful stained-glass windows surround the chapel. It was built as a private place to meditate.

KENTUCKY

1. **Hodgenville, Kentucky**
   Birthplace: Abraham Lincoln
   Boyhood Home: Abraham Lincoln
   Presidential Museum: Abraham Lincoln

2. **Louisville, Kentucky**
   Family Home: Zachary Taylor
   Final Resting Place: Zachary Taylor

Hodgenville, Kentucky

Abraham Lincoln
Birthplace
Open to the public
Abraham Lincoln Birthplace National Historic Park[37]
National Park Service
2995 Lincoln Farm Road
Hodgenville, Kentucky 42748

The park is open daily from 8:00 a.m. to 4:30 p.m. The visitor center closes at 4:00 p.m., and the park is closed on Thanksgiving, Christmas, and New Year's Day.

Abraham Lincoln was born on February 12, 1809, in a log cabin in Hodgenville, Kentucky. This was his home for the first two years of his life. On the site of his birth, this reconstructed cabin is enclosed in the Memorial Building that was constructed from 1909 to 1911. View the Sinking Springs and the Memorial Building. Walk up the fifty-six steps (that you will count) commemorating the fifty-six years of Lincoln's life, and watch a film in a small museum in the visitor center. While in Hodgenville, stop by the nearby Lincoln's Boyhood Home at Knob Creek, where Lincoln lived from age two until he was eight years old.

---

[37] https://nps.gov/abli/index.htm

Hodgenville, Kentucky

Abraham Lincoln
Boyhood Home
Open to the public
Abraham Lincoln's Boyhood Home at Knob Creek[38]
National Park Service
7120 Bardstown Road
Hodgenville, Kentucky 42748

Open from 8:30 a.m. to 4:30 p.m. Start at the Abraham Lincoln Birthplace National Historic Park Visitor Center for your tour.

The Lincoln Family moved to this home when Lincoln was two years old. They lived in this farmhouse from 1811 to 1816. Lincoln stated, "My earliest recollection is of the Knob Creek place." The original cabin no longer exists, but the reconstructed cabin has period furnishings as it would have when the Lincoln family lived here.

---

[38] https://www.nps.gov/abli/planyourvisit/boyhood-home.htm

Susan Alba

Hodgenville, Kentucky

Abraham Lincoln
Presidential Museum
Open to the public
Abraham Lincoln Museum
66 Lincoln Square
Hodgenville, Kentucky 42748

Open Mondays through Saturdays from 8:30 a.m. to 4:30 p.m. and on Sundays from 12:30 p.m. to 4:30 p.m.

This very well-done museum has two floors of dioramas with life-size wax figures set up in scenes depicting Abraham Lincoln's life from his birth in a log cabin to the scene in Ford's Theater. There are also artifacts from the Civil War on display. You'll find Lincoln memorabilia as well as many local-made crafts in the museum gift shop.

Louisville, Kentucky

Zachary Taylor
Family Home
Not open to the public
Springfield
5608 Apache Road
Louisville, Kentucky 40207

A half mile from Zachary Taylor National Cemetery is the family home of Zachary Taylor. The original house was built in the 1790s, then was added on to in the 1810s, becoming the two-and-a-half-story brick home that stands today. Taylor lived here for twenty years of his life. There is a marker in front of the home, but it is a private residence.

Louisville, Kentucky

Zachary Taylor
Final Resting Place
Open to the public
Zachary Taylor National Cemetery[39]
4701 Brownsboro Road
Louisville, Kentucky 40207

Open daily from 8:00 a.m. to 4:30 p.m.

Zachary Taylor died on July 9, 1850, in his bed at the White House from complications with cholera. He was buried in a temporary grave in the Congressional Burial Ground Cemetery and was later moved into a private family cemetery. In 1926, the United States erected this neoclassical-style building of marble with glass-paneled bronze doors. Taylor and his wife were reinterred again into their final resting place in the Zachary Taylor National Cemetery, which is in the National Register of Historic Places.

---

[39] http://www.cem.va.gov/cems/nchp/zacharytaylor.asp

MAINE

1. **Kennebunkport, Maine**
Family Home: George H. W. Bush
St. Ann's Episcopal Church: George H. W. Bush

Kennebunkport, Maine

George H. W. Bush
Family Home
Not open to the public
Walker's Point
Ocean Avenue
Kennebunkport, Maine 04046

The Bush family bought this home in Kennebunkport, Maine, in 1901. The large estate sits overlooking the Atlantic Ocean on beautiful Walker's Point. View the house from an overlook on Ocean Avenue, where you can see a marker and anchor to honor the former president.

Kennebunkport, Maine

George H. W. Bush
St. Ann's Episcopal Church
Open to the public
Walker's Point
167 Ocean Avenue
Kennebunkport, Maine 04046

This is the church of the Bush family in Kennebunkport, Maine. During the summer, there are sunrise services on the lawn overlooking the ocean.

This historic seaside stone chapel on the coast of Maine was built in 1887. Special services are held outside on the park grounds. I had to mention this church because my husband and I attended an outdoor service here during one of our visits to Kennebunkport. As we were sitting waiting for the service to begin, my husband pointed out people filing into the row in front of us. It was President George H. W. Bush, his wife Barbara Bush, and some other family members. Afterward, we got to meet and briefly speak to the president.

MASSACHUSETTS

1. **Boston, Massachusetts**
   Presidential Library and Museum: John F. Kennedy

2. **Brookline, Massachusetts**
   Birthplace: John F. Kennedy

3. **Hyannis, Massachusetts**
   Museum: John F. Kennedy

4. **Milton, Massachusetts**
   Birthplace: George H. W. Bush

5. **Northampton, Massachusetts**
   Presidential Library and Museum: Calvin Coolidge

6. **Quincy, Massachusetts**
   Adams National Historical Park
   Birthplace: John Adams
   Birthplace: John Quincy Adams
   Final Resting Place: John Adams
   Final Resting Place: John Quincy Adams
   Family Home: John Adams

Boston, Massachusetts

John F. Kennedy
Presidential Library and Museum
Open to the public
JFK Presidential Library[40]
Administered by the National Archives and Records Administration
Columbia Point
220 Morrissey Boulevard
Boston, Massachusetts 02125

Open daily from 9:00 a.m. to 5:00 p.m., with the last film showing at 3:55 p.m. The Museum Café is open from 9:00 a.m. to 5:00 p.m. Closed on Thanksgiving, Christmas, and New Year's Day.

Start with an introductory film to learn about the life of JFK. Visit many displays, including the Briefing Room, Space Race, the Oval Office Exhibit, and the First Lady Exhibit. View gifts from dignitaries from many countries as well as many changing exhibitions. See photos and personal belongings of the Kennedy family. Visit the gift shop and Museum Café. End your tour in the glass pavilion.

My husband particularly enjoyed the glass pavilion overlooking Boston Harbor at the end of the tour. This room is where you can view Kennedy's Profile in Courage Award. The large glass enclosure is empty, at the request of Jackie Kennedy, so the visitor can reflect on what they've seen and the unfinished life of JFK.

---

[40] https://www.jfklibrary.org/

Brookline, Massachusetts

John F. Kennedy
Birthplace
Open to the public
John Fitzgerald Kennedy National Historic Site[41]
National Park Service
83 Beals Street
Brookline, Massachusetts 02446

Open Wednesdays through Sundays from 9:30 a.m. to 5:00 p.m. from May 21 through October 30.

This quaint three-story, nine-room Colonial-style home on Beals Street has been restored with the help of Kennedy's mother, Rose Fitzgerald Kennedy. John Fitzgerald Kennedy was born on May 29, 1917, in the second-story master bedroom. The furnishings are replicated as closely as possible to how they looked in 1917. When you visit, you can tour the house and look into all of the rooms, including the room and bed where Kennedy was born. You can also view a short film and visit a gift shop on the lower level of the house. There's a historical marker in the front that reads:

BIRTHPLACE OF JOHN F. KENNEDY
35th President of the United States
Born May 29, 1917 on this site
83 Beals Street Brookline, Mass
This commemorative plaque erected by
Town of Brookline, Mass
on September 12, 1961

---

[41] https://www.nps.gov/jofi/index.htm

Hyannis, Massachusetts

John F. Kennedy
Museum
Open to the public
John F. Kennedy Hyannis Museum[42]
397 Main Street
Hyannis, Massachusetts 02601
Kennedy Compound
50 Merchant Ave.
Hyannis, Massachusetts 02601

Open from mid-April through November on Mondays through Saturdays from 10:00 a.m. to 4:00 p.m. and on Sundays from noon to 4:00 p.m. Closed from December to mid-April.

This museum is small but well-done, with a collection of photos and short films showing the legacy of President Kennedy's family, their love of Cape Cod, and their summers sailing on the ocean at the Kennedy Compound. Learn about the public and private life of John F. Kennedy. I enjoyed the two special exhibits on display during my visit: Rose Kennedy, a small rose-colored room about the life of Kennedy's mother, and the Bobby Exhibit, which told the story of the close Kennedy brothers. There is a small John F. Kennedy Museum gift shop.

[42] http://jfkhyannismuseum.org/

Milton, Massachusetts

George H. W. Bush
Birthplace
Not open to the public
173 Adams Street
Milton, Massachusetts 02186

The fifteen-room Victorian-style home is now a private residence. Although it is difficult to see the house, it is worth the short drive from the Adams National Historical Park to see the home where George Herbert Walker Bush was born on June 12, 1924, in a room on the second floor. Coincidentally, he was born on a street named for John Adams and John Quincy Adams, who once lived on the same road. At the corner in front of the house, there's a historic stone marker that reads:

173 Adams Street
Milton, Massachusetts
Birthplace of
GEORGE HERBERT WALKER BUSH
June 12, 1924
Forty-first President of
The United States of America

Northampton, Massachusetts

Calvin Coolidge
Presidential Library
Open to the public
Calvin Coolidge Presidential Library and Museum[43]
20 West Street
Northampton, Massachusetts 01060

Open Mondays through Fridays from 10:00 a.m. to 5:00 p.m. and on Saturdays from 2:00 p.m. to 4:00 p.m. Closed on Sundays.

This library houses manuscripts, artifacts, and exhibits from Coolidge's life. There are documents for research, speeches, and personal letters ranging from the White House years to after his presidency. On display is the "electric exercise horse" Coolidge used. The research library is housed in Forbes Library, making it the only Presidential Library and Museum to be in a public library. Albeit only a one-room museum, it is quite nice, with a friendly and knowledgeable staff.

---

[43] http://forbeslibrary.org/calvin-coolidge-presidential-library-and-museum/

Quincy, Massachusetts

Adams National Historical Park
Open to the public
National Park Service Visitors Center[44]
1250 Hancock Street
Quincy, Massachusetts 02169

The Galleria at Presidents Place will need to be your first stop. Here, you purchase tickets for tours of all of the Adams's homes. A trolley will take you to each location. The park is open daily from April 19 to November 10 from 9:00 a.m. to 5:00 p.m.

    This is where your tour of the presidential family's homes begins. There is a gift shop and a small theater where you can view a short film about the generations of the Adams family. The trolley stops at the visitor center, and then it will take you to tour the John Adams Birthplace, the John Quincy Adams Birthplace, the Old House at Peace field, and the Stone Library.

---

[44] https://www.nps.gov/adam/index.htm

Susan Alba

Quincy, Massachusetts

John Adams
Birthplace
Open to the public
John Adams Birthplace
133 Franklin Street
Quincy, Massachusetts 02169

The nation's oldest presidential birthplace, this house was built in 1681 on what was formerly named "Old Coast Road," which ran between Boston and Plymouth. The John Adams Birthplace used some of the materials from the original structure built on this property around 1650. It was originally constructed as a saltbox-style home, with two lower rooms and two upper rooms built around a massive central fireplace. With the renovations over the years, the home now has nine rooms. Adams's father, Deacon John Adams Sr., farmed here in the summer and made shoes in the winter. Adams was born on October 30, 1735, and spent his childhood here. When John Adams married Abigail Smith, they moved into the adjacent home, where another president was born: John Quincy Adams.

Quincy, Massachusetts

John Quincy Adams
Birthplace
Open to the public
John Quincy Adams Birthplace[45]
141 Franklin Street
Quincy, Massachusetts 02169

This house is only seventy-five feet away from the John Adams Birthplace and is also part of the Adams National Historical Park.

When John Adams married Abigail Smith, they built and moved into the house next door to John Adams's birthplace, where their son, John Quincy Adams, was born on July 11, 1767, in the front east chamber. The house was built in 1716, and like John Adams's birthplace, it's also a saltbox-style home. It was in this house, in the northeast corner office, that John Adams drafted the Constitution of Massachusetts.

---

[45] https://www.nps.gov/adam/index.htm

Quincy, Massachusetts

Adams Family Home
Open to the public
The Old House at Peace field and the Stone Library[46]
135 Adams Street
Quincy, Massachusetts 02169

---

[46] https://www.nps.gov/adam/index.htm

This home, built in 1731, was the residence of four generations of the Adams family, including John and Abigail and John Quincy and Louisa Catherine Adams. The Old House has many original artifacts on display.

The Stone Library was built in 1870 to house the over twelve thousand volumes of books and documents that belonged to the Adams families. Surrounded by beautiful gardens, the fireproof structure is separate from the Old House at Peace field.

Quincy, Massachusetts

John Adams
Final Resting Place
Open to the public
United First Parish Church
1306 Hancock Street
Quincy, Massachusetts 02169

John Adams died in his home at Peacefield on July 4, 1826, at 6:20 p.m.—the same day as Thomas Jefferson. However, Adams was not aware that Jefferson had died just hours before. On his deathbed, he said, "Thomas Jefferson survives." Adams and Jefferson hadn't spoken for many years and had just rekindled their friendship. Adams was buried in a tomb at the Hancock Cemetery across the street from the United First Parish Church in what is now Quincy. In 1828, Adams's body was reinterred into the crypt in the basement of the United First Parish Church. The fifteen-star flag (1795–1818) is draped over his granite coffin.

The parish first gathered in the year 1636, was established in 1639, and the church structure was built in 1828. There is a guided tour of the church and crypt. Here, you can enter the crypt to view the tombs of John Adams and his wife Abigail Adams as well as John Quincy Adams and his wife Louisa Catherine Adams.

Quincy, Massachusetts

John Quincy Adams
Final Resting Place
Open to the public
United First Parish Church
1306 Hancock Street
Quincy, Massachusetts 02169

John Quincy Adams died on February 23, 1848, at the Capitol Building in Washington D.C. After many days of travel and funeral services, Adams was buried in the family vault at Hancock Cemetery, just as his father had been. In 1852, he was moved to his final resting place in the basement of the United First Parish Church next to his father. The twenty-four-star flag (1822–1836) is draped over his granite coffin.

MICHIGAN

1. **Ann Arbor, Michigan**
   Presidential Library: Gerald R. Ford

2. **Grand Rapids, Michigan**
   Presidential Museum: Gerald R. Ford
   Final Resting Place: Gerald R. Ford

Ann Arbor, Michigan

Gerald R. Ford
Presidential Library
Open to the public
Gerald R. Ford Presidential Library[47]
Administered by the National Archives and Records Administration
University of Michigan
1000 Beal Avenue
Ann Arbor, Michigan 48109

This library has videos, publications, and many exhibits, including a timeline on the lives of Gerald and Betty Ford. You can also visit the private office used by Ford during his presidency. From here, it is a 130-mile drive to the museum in Grand Rapids, Michigan.

---

[47] https://www.fordlibrarymuseum.gov/visit-library.aspx

Grand Rapids, Michigan

Gerald R. Ford
Presidential Museum
Open to the public
Gerald R. Ford Presidential Museum[48]
Administered by the National Archives and Records Administration
303 Pearl Street NW
Grand Rapids, Michigan 49504

Open Mondays through Saturdays from 9:00 a.m. to 5:00 p.m. and on Sundays from noon to 5:00 p.m. Closed on Thanksgiving, Christmas, and New Year's Day.

This museum has exhibits, programs, and events. It opened in 1982, and there are displays highlighting Ford's life from his early years through his presidency. There is also a museum store.

---

[48] https://www.fordlibrarymuseum.gov

Grand Rapids, Michigan

Gerald R. Ford
Final Resting Place
Open to the public
Gerald R. Ford Presidential Museum
Administered by the National Archives and Records Administration
303 Pearl Street NW
Grand Rapids, Michigan 49504

Gerald R. Ford died on December 6, 2006, at the age of ninety-three. The burial site of the president and his wife, Betty B. Ford, is on the grounds of the Gerald R. Ford Presidential Library and Museum in Grand Rapids, Michigan.

MISSISSIPPI

1. **Starkville, Mississippi**
   Presidential Library: Ulysses S. Grant

Starkville, Mississippi

Ulysses S. Grant
Presidential Library and Museum
Open to the public
Ulysses S. Grant Presidential Library[49]
449 Hardy Road
Starkville, Mississippi 39759

Open Mondays through Fridays from 7:30 a.m. to 5:00 p.m. and on Saturdays from 10:00 a.m. to 2:00 p.m. Closed on Sundays and school vacations.

The library is on the fourth floor of the Mitchell Memorial Library on the campus of the Mississippi State University and has the largest collection of artifacts, memoirs, photographs, and memorabilia of Grant. It has mementos from his childhood, his important role during the Civil War, his time as president, and his life after being president. See his memoirs written and completed just before his death. The library also houses a large collection dedicated to Abraham Lincoln.

[49] usgrantlibrary.org

MISSOURI

1. **Grandview, Missouri**
   Family Home: Harry S. Truman

2. **Independence, Missouri**
   Family Home: Harry S. Truman
   Final Resting Place: Harry S. Truman
   Presidential Library and Museum: Harry S. Truman

3. **Lamar, Missouri**
   Birthplace: Harry S. Truman

4. **St. Louis, Missouri**
   Family Home: Ulysses S. Grant

Grandview, Missouri

Harry S. Truman
Family Home
Not open to the public
Truman Farm Home
12301 Blue Ridge Boulevard
Grandview, Missouri 64030

The Truman Farm Home, also known as the Solomon Young Farm, was built in 1894, originally on a six-hundred-acre working farm. The home didn't have plumbing or heating. The Truman family moved here in 1887, and Truman spent eleven years working the farm. The house on the remaining ten acres is part of the Harry S. Truman Natural Historic Site. The farmhouse is not open to the public, although the grounds are open.

Independence, Missouri

Harry S. Truman
Presidential Library and Museum
Open to the public
Harry S. Truman Presidential Library and Museum[50]
Administered by the National Archives and Records Administration
500 West U.S. Highway 24
Independence, Missouri 64050

Open Mondays through Saturdays 9:00 a.m. to 5:00 p.m. and on Sundays from noon to 5:00 p.m.

The Harry S. Truman Presidential Library and Museum has exhibits that reflect the life and times of Truman during his years in office. View manuscripts and photos from World War II. Watch videos and hear audio recordings of Truman's life from his boyhood, family, military, and time with his wife, Bess.

---

[50] https://www.trumanlibrary.gov

Independence, Missouri

Harry S. Truman
Family Home
Open to the public
Truman Home
National Park Service
219 North Delaware Street
Independence, Missouri 64050

Open daily from 9:00 a.m. to 4:30 p.m. Closed on Mondays. Start at the visitor center at 233 North Main St.

When Truman married, he and his wife Bess moved into her family home. This was the Summer White House during Truman's presidency. It was where Truman resided after his presidency, and it remains exactly as it did when he lived here. This house and other family homes are open for tours.

Independence, Missouri

Harry S. Truman
Final Resting Place
Open to the public
Harry S. Truman Presidential Library and Museum
Administered by the National Archives and Records Administration
500 West U.S. Highway 24
Independence, Missouri 64050

Open Mondays through Saturdays from 9:00 a.m. to 5:00 p.m. and on Sundays from noon to 5:00 p.m.

Visit the graves of Harry and Bess Truman. Harry Truman's grave is in the courtyard outside of the Harry S. Truman Presidential Library and Museum. He chose this spot, which was originally outside of his office.

Lamar, Missouri

Harry S. Truman
Birthplace
Open to the public
Harry S. Truman Birthplace
State Historic Site
1009 Truman Street
Lamar, Missouri 64759

Open March through October on Wednesdays through Saturdays from 10:00 a.m. to 4:00 p.m. Open on Sundays from noon to 4:00 p.m. Open November through February from 10:00 a.m. to 4:00 p.m. on Wednesdays through Saturdays. Closed Easter, Thanksgiving, Christmas, and New Year's Day.

On May 8, 1884, Harry S. Truman was born in this small twenty-by-twenty-eight-foot frame farmhouse. You can view the home with furnishings that reflect what living in Missouri would have been like in Truman's time. Here, you can see the downstairs bedroom where Truman was born; the room is marked with a plaque. There is a historical marker on the grounds in front of the home.

St. Louis, Missouri

Ulysses S. Grant
Family Home
Open to the public
Ulysses S. Grant National Historic Site
National Park Service
7400 Grant Road
St. Louis, Missouri 63123

Open daily from 9:00 a.m. to 5:00 p.m. Closed on Thanksgiving, Christmas, and New Year's Day.

This home, also known as White Haven, is where Grant met his future wife, Julia Dent. After their marriage, he lived here with her family. Learn about Grant's military career and his years in the White House.

Tours begin at the visitor center with the film *Ulysses S. Grant: A Legacy of Freedom*. Then, take a guided tour of Grant and Julia's home. Stroll through the grounds and several buildings on the property, including the stone building and the horse stables that Grant built. Visit the museum in the stable to learn of Grant's life in Missouri. Stop in the bookstore for unique gifts and books, to view a film about Ulysses S. Grant, and to speak to the friendly, knowledgeable staff.

Another home of Grant's is Hardscrabble, one that he built for Julia and their children with the help of the family slaves. The Hardscrabble building is now located on Grant's Farm, part of the nearby Anheuser-Busch property adjacent to Ulysses S. Grant National Historic Site.

NEBRASKA

1. **Omaha, Nebraska**
   Birthplace: Gerald R. Ford

Omaha, Nebraska

Gerald R. Ford
Birthplace
Open to the public
Gerald R. Ford Birthsite and Gardens[51]
3202 Woolworth Avenue
Omaha, Nebraska 68105

The birthplace and gardens are administered by the city of Omaha, and the lovely gardens are open to the public daily from early morning until dusk.

Gerald R. Ford, born Leslie L. King Jr., was born on July 14, 1913, in a three-story, fourteen-room Victorian house. The home, built in 1893, had belonged to his grandparents. The original structure was destroyed by a fire. The site features presidential mementos, an information kiosk, a fountain, and a garden of roses and flowers complete with a colonnade in honor of former First Lady Betty Ford. There is a model of the original home and a memorial marker.

---

[51] http://www.nebraskahistory.org/conserve/brthsite.htm

NEW HAMPSHIRE

1. **Concord, New Hampshire**
   Family Home: Franklin Pierce
   Final Resting Place: Franklin Pierce

2. **Hillsborough, New Hampshire**
   Birthplace: Franklin Pierce
   Childhood Home: Franklin Pierce

Concord, New Hampshire

Franklin Pierce
Family Home
Open to the public
Pierce Manse[52]
14 Horseshoe Pond Lane
Concord, New Hampshire 03301

Open June through September on Tuesdays through Saturdays from 11:00 a.m. to 3:00 p.m., and September and October on Fridays and Saturdays from noon to 3:00 p.m.

The Pierce Manse is a historical museum that was the home of Franklin Pierce, his wife Jane, and their two sons from 1842–1848. The home is full of artifacts so that you can learn about his life in the mid-19th century. The Pierce Manse is the only home ever owned and lived in by Franklin Pierce.

Note: This is one of the homes that had touring hours on the web page but was closed when we arrived. Be sure to call for hours.

---

[52] http://www.piercemanse.org/

Concord, New Hampshire

President Franklin Pierce
Final Resting Place
Open to the public
Old North Cemetery
137 North State Street
Concord, New Hampshire 03301

The cemetery is open from dawn until dusk. A marker at the entrance of the cemetery reads:

Franklin Pierce
1804–1869
Fourteenth President of the United States
(1853–1857)
Lies buried in nearby Minot enclosure
Native son of New Hampshire,
graduate of Bowdoin College,
lawyer, effective political leader,
Congressman and U.S. Senator,
Mexican War veteran, courageous
advocate of States' Rights,
he was popularly known as
"Young Hickory of the Granite Hills."

Hillsborough, New Hampshire

Franklin Pierce
Birthplace
Franklin Pierce Lake

Franklin Pierce Lake, also known as the Jackman Reservoir, is located off of the Franklin Pierce Highway in Hillsborough County, New Hampshire. The log cabin Pierce had been born in on November 23, 1804, was submerged underwater in 1926 for the dam and reservoir to be built. Pierce grew up in the nearby Franklin Pierce Homestead.

Hillsborough, New Hampshire

Franklin Pierce
Childhood Home
Open to the public
Hillsborough Historical Society
301 2nd NH Turnpike
Hillsborough, New Hampshire 03244

Open Memorial Day weekend through Labor Day on Fridays through Tuesdays (closed Wednesdays and Thursdays), and on Saturdays and Sundays in September and October, closing for the season on Columbus Day. Operating hours are from 10:00 a.m. to 4:00 p.m.

This elegant, stately home began as a tavern run by Pierce's father. The family moved in shortly after Pierce's birth. Pierce lived here through his childhood and returned after attending law school. The house has some of the original wallpaper and stenciling. You will also see many items that belonged to the family. A marker reads:

PIERCE HOMESTEAD
The Pierce Homestead was built in
1904 by Benjamin Pierce, a general
in the American Revolution twice
governor of New Hampshire (1827–28,
1829–30), and father of Franklin Pierce,
the 14th President of the United States (1853–57).
Franklin Pierce was born in Hillsboro
November 23, 1804 and the family occupied
this dwelling shortly thereafter.

NEW JERSEY

1. **Caldwell, New Jersey**
   Birthplace: Grover Cleveland

2. **Morristown, New Jersey**
   Headquarters: George Washington
   Museum: George Washington

3. **Princeton, New Jersey**
   Family Home: Grover Cleveland
   Final Resting Place: Grover Cleveland

Caldwell, New Jersey

Stephen Grover Cleveland
Birthplace
Open to the public
Grover Cleveland Birthplace State Historic Site[53]
Grover Cleveland Park
207 Bloomfield Avenue
Caldwell, New Jersey 07006

Open year-round Wednesdays through Sundays from 10:00 a.m. to noon and from 1:00 p.m. to 4:00 p.m. Closed on holidays.

Stephen Grover Cleveland was born here on March 18, 1837. The home has been restored to how it would have looked then. Built in 1832, the manse contains many of his personal possessions and original furnishings and artifacts, including Cleveland's cradle. It is the only museum in the country dedicated to Cleveland's life. Cleveland is the only president who served two non-consecutive terms.

---

[53] https://www.nps.gov/nr/travel/presidents/grover_cleveland_birthplace.html

Morristown, New Jersey

George Washington
Headquarters
Open to the public
Washington's Headquarters Museum
Morristown National Historical Park
National Park Service
30 Washington Place
Morristown, New Jersey 07960

Open daily from 10:00 a.m. to 4:00 p.m. Closed on Thanksgiving, Christmas, and New Year's Day.

The Jacob Ford Jr. home is the oldest home museum in the United States. When Ford died in 1777, his widow allowed George Washington to use the house as his headquarters from 1779 to 1780. She and her children stayed in only two of the rooms during Washington's stay. The home is decorated as it may have appeared during that time. The Visitor Center Museum was constructed to resemble Mount Vernon. Here, you can watch a film about George Washington and the Morris County Militia and view the large collection of historical artifacts from the Revolutionary War. There are two gift shops: one in the headquarters and the other in the visitor center, where the tours begin.

During the Revolutionary War, while George Washington stayed in Morristown, he frequently traveled to nearby Maplewood. During some visits, he'd stop at the home of Timothy and Esther Ball. Esther was believed to be Washington's cousin. The Timothy Ball House on Ridgewood Road in Maplewood is one of several houses in N.J. that can claim: "George Washington slept here."

Princeton, New Jersey

Grover Cleveland
Family Home
Not open to the public
National Park Service
Westland[54]
15 Hodge Road
Princeton, New Jersey 08540

Grover Cleveland married Frances Folsom in the White House while serving as president. During his last year as president, he bought this two-and-a-half-story home in Princeton for them. Cleveland named it Westland. He died here on June 24, 1908. Westland is a private residence and is not open to the public.

---

[54] https://www.nps.gov/nr/travel/presidents/grover_cleveland_home.html

Princeton, New Jersey

Grover Cleveland
Final Resting Place
Open to the public
Princeton Cemetery
29 Greenview Avenue
Princeton, New Jersey 08540

Open daily from 9:00 a.m. to 5:00 p.m.

Grover Cleveland died on June 24, 1908. He was buried in a small cemetery in his hometown, not far from his birthplace. Princeton Cemetery, established in 1757, is referred to as "The Westminster Abbey of the United States." Also buried with Cleveland are his wife Frances and his daughter Baby Ruth, who died at age twelve. Vice President Aaron Burr is also buried in this cemetery.

NEW YORK

1. **Albany, New York**
   Final Resting Place: Chester A. Arthur

2. **Buffalo, New York**
   Inaugural Site: Theodore Roosevelt
   Final Resting Place: Millard Fillmore

3. **East Aurora, New York**
   Family Home: Millard Fillmore

4. **Hyde Park, New York**
   Birthplace: Franklin Delano Roosevelt
   Presidential Library and Museum: Franklin Delano Roosevelt
   Final Resting Place: Franklin Delano Roosevelt

5. **Kinderhook, New York**
   Birthplace: Martin Van Buren
   Family Home: Martin Van Buren
   Final Resting Place: Martin Van Buren

6. **Moravia, New York**
   Birthplace: Millard Fillmore
   Birthplace Replica: Millard Fillmore

7. **New York, New York**
   Family Home: Chester A. Arthur
   Final Resting Place: Ulysses S. Grant
   Birthplace: Theodore Roosevelt
   Family Home: Donald Trump

8. **Oyster Bay, New York**
   Family Home: Theodore Roosevelt
   Final Resting Place: Theodore Roosevelt

9. **Richmond Hill, New York**
   Birthplace: Donald Trump

10. **Wilton, New York**
    Grant Cottage: Ulysses S. Grant

Albany, New York

Chester A. Arthur
Final Resting Place
Open to the public
Albany Rural Cemetery[55]
National Register of Historic Places
Cemetery Avenue
Albany, New York 12204

Open daily from 7:30 a.m. to 4:30 p.m. and until 7:00 p.m. during daylight saving time.

Chester Arthur died on November 18, 1886. He's buried just outside of Albany beside his wife in the Albany Rural Cemetery, a beautiful rural graveyard with winding roads and gorgeous monuments. The Angel of Sorrow is placing a palm on Arthur's sarcophagus. The cemetery is on the National Register of Historic Places.

---

[55] http://albanyruralcemetery.org/

Buffalo, New York

Theodore Roosevelt
Inaugural Site
Open to the public
Theodore Roosevelt Inaugural National Historic Site[56]
641 Delaware Avenue
Buffalo, New York 14202

Open for tours Mondays through Fridays from 9:00 a.m. to 5:00 p.m. and on Saturdays and Sundays from noon to 5:00 p.m. Closed on holidays.

Theodore Roosevelt took the oath of office for president of the United States in the library of this house following the assassination of President William McKinley. Tour the home and stand in the library where the historic event took place. Original architectural features of the home were recreated using photographs from the early 1900s. Walk through and see the reconstructed rooms and interactive exhibits. Visit the museum gift shop that has a wide variety of unique Theodore Roosevelt-themed items.

[56] https://www.trsite.org/

Buffalo, New York

Millard Fillmore
Final Resting Place
Open to the public
Forest Lawn Cemetery and Garden[57]
National Register of Historic Places
1411 Delaware Avenue
Buffalo, New York 14209

Open in the spring from 8:00 a.m. to 7:00 p.m. and in the fall from 8:00 a.m. to 5:00 p.m.

Millard Fillmore died on March 8, 1874. He is buried in Forest Lawn Cemetery beside his wife, Abigail, in the Fillmore family plot. The grave is marked with an impressive twenty-two-foot monument enclosed by an iron fence. This beautiful cemetery with fountains, lakes, and streams has trolley tours and many scheduled events.

---

[57] http://www.forest-lawn.com/

East Aurora, New York

Millard Fillmore
Family Home
Open to the public
Millard Fillmore Museum
24 Shearer Avenue
East Aurora, New York 14052

Open from Memorial Day through October on Wednesdays and on weekends. Tours are from 1:00 p.m. to 4:00 p.m.

Millard Fillmore and his wife Abigail built this home in the 1820s and stayed here until 1830. The house was moved and restored to its 1820s decor in the 1930s. It is now decorated with some of the Fillmores's furnishings from other homes, including some furniture they owned in the White House.

Hyde Park, New York

Franklin Delano Roosevelt
Birthplace
Open to the public
Home of Franklin D. Roosevelt National Historic Site[58]
National Park Service
Springwood Estate
4097 Albany Post Road
Hyde Park, New York 12538

Open year-round, seven days a week. Closed on Thanksgiving, Christmas, and New Year's Day.

Franklin Delano Roosevelt was born on January 30, 1882, in the second-floor bedroom at Springwood Estate, the family home in Hyde Park. The house was built around 1800 and was bought by Roosevelt's father in 1867. After his father died, Franklin and his mother continued to live at the estate. When Franklin married Eleanor in 1905, they moved into the house with Franklin's mother. During a tour, you can see the bedroom he was born in, the room Roosevelt used as a boy, the living room, the library, and a variety of items collected by Roosevelt. The estate is part of the Presidential Library and Museum.

---

[58] https://www.nps.gov/hofr/index.htm

Hyde Park, New York

Franklin Delano Roosevelt
Presidential Library and Museum
Open to the public
Franklin D. Roosevelt Presidential Library and Museum
Administered by the National Archives and Records Administration
4097 Albany Post Road
Hyde Park, New York 12538

Open year-round from 9:00 a.m. to 5:00 p.m. Closed on Thanksgiving and Christmas.

President Roosevelt donated this estate to the American people. When the family relinquished the rights to the property, it was transferred to the Department of the Interior. The beautiful 290-acre site on the Hudson River is open to the public. Tour the visitor center, the FDR Library, the Springwood Estate, the museum, the Coach House and Stables, the gravesite, and the beautiful grounds of President Roosevelt's home. Roosevelt planned the library while serving as president. Opened in 1941, it was the first Presidential Library. He wanted a place to preserve his books and important papers. It is also where he had four of his fireside chats. View papers, books, photos, gifts, and videos of the president and Eleanor, and visit the nearby Val-Kill Cottage at the Eleanor Roosevelt National Historic Site.

Hyde Park, New York

Franklin Delano Roosevelt
Final Resting Place
Open to the public
Home of Franklin D. Roosevelt National Historic Site[59]
National Park Service
4097 Albany Post Road
Hyde Park, New York 12538

The Rose Garden was one of FDR's favorite places, which is why he chose this as his final resting place. Franklin and Eleanor Roosevelt are buried in the beautiful gardens on the estate.

---

[59] https://www.nps.gov/hofr/index.htm

Kinderhook, New York

Martin Van Buren
Family Home
Open to the public
Lindenwald
Martin Van Buren National Historic Site[60]
National Park Service
1013 Old Post Road
Kinderhook, New York 12106

Open from May through October daily from 9:00 a.m. to 4:30 p.m. Open weekends only during November until December 5. Closed from December 6 until May.

Lindenwald was built in 1719, and Van Buren bought the property in 1839 to restore it as a place to retire after his presidency. It is open to the public and has guided tours of the mansion. Lindenwald will provide an opportunity to experience the tastes, lifestyle, and many roles of Van Buren. It reflects life after his presidency—you will see his law books, political documents, portraits, and even cartoons of himself that he displayed. Visit the grounds where he tended to his gardens of vegetables and flowers. The tours begin in the National Park Service Visitor Center, where there is a short video and a small gift shop.

---

[60] https://www.nps.gov/mava/index.htm

Kinderhook, New York

Martin Van Buren
Birthplace
Not open to the public
46 Hudson Street[61]
Kinderhook, New York 12106

The original home where Martin Van Buren was born on December 5, 1782, had been a tavern on the family farm. The original house was torn down and no longer exists. Van Buren spent his youth there. The site was sold and is now a private residence. There is a marker on the roadside at the site.

---

[61] https://www.nps.gov/mava/index.htm

Kinderhook, New York

Martin Van Buren
Final Resting Place
Open to the public
Kinderhook Village Cemetery
Albany Avenue and Kindertree Drive
Kinderhook, New York 12106

Open daily from 7:00 a.m. until sunset.

Martin Van Buren died in his home at Lindenwald on July 24, 1862. He is buried next to his wife in the Kinderhook Village Cemetery, not far from the Van Buren home. The marker and fifteen-foot granite stone are in the cemetery on Albany Avenue.

Moravia, New York

Millard Fillmore
Birthplace
Open to the public
Millard Fillmore Birthplace
Fillmore Road
Moravia, New York 13118

In a secluded spot on a back road in the woods, there is a picnic area and pavilion at Fillmore's original birth site. The footprint of the log-cabin home is marked by a flower garden. The historical marker is on the roadside.

Moravia, New York

Millard Fillmore
Birthplace Replica
Open to the public
Millard Fillmore Birthplace
Fillmore Glen State Park
1686 NY 38
Moravia, New York 13118

The park is open from dawn until dusk daily. The log cabin is open Wednesdays through Sundays from 8:00 a.m. until dusk.

In Fillmore Glen State Park, there is a replica of the log cabin where Millard Fillmore was born on January 7, 1800. The original cabin was destroyed in 1851, but the replica has furnishings that are an example of what they would have been in 1800. The model is actually five miles from the real birthplace.

New York, New York

Chester A. Arthur
Family Home
Not open to the public
Chester A. Arthur House
National Park Service
123 Lexington Avenue
New York, New York 10016

This four-story brownstone townhouse was home to Chester Arthur before and after his presidency. After President Garfield's death, Arthur privately took the oath of office in this New York home. It is now a privately owned building with a commercial business on the first floor and is not open to the public. There is a bronze historical plaque on the building.

New York, New York

Ulysses S. Grant
Final Resting Place
Open to the public
General Grant National Memorial
West 122nd Street & Riverside Drive
New York, New York 10027

Grant's tomb is open year-round Wednesdays through Sundays from 9:00 a.m. to 5:00 p.m. and is closed on Mondays and Tuesdays.

Ulysses S. Grant died July 23, 1885, at Mount McGregor, the home of a friend, just north of Saratoga Springs, New York. He died at sixty-three years old from throat cancer. Following his death, there were several services and funeral processions. Many days later, his body traveled on the train from Saratoga Springs to New York City, making multiple stops for crowds of people to pay their respects. Guards accompanied his body until it finally arrived in New York City on August 12 to a tomb in Riverside Park. Eventually, a new tomb was constructed. Grant's body was carefully transferred from the temporary vault twelve years later, on April 17, 1897. The visitor center and gift shop are open, where you can purchase memorabilia and publications.

New York, New York

Theodore Roosevelt
Birthplace
Open to the public
Theodore Roosevelt Birthplace National Historic Site[62]
National Park Service
28 East 20th Street
New York, New York 10003

Open Tuesdays through Saturdays from 9:00 a.m. to 5:00 p.m. Closed on Sundays, Mondays, and on Thanksgiving and Christmas.

From his birth on October 27, 1858, until 1872, Theodore Roosevelt was raised in this townhouse in New York City. The original home was destroyed in 1916. The site was rebuilt and decorated with many of the original furnishings provided by Roosevelt's sisters and wife. Inside, you will tour five rooms with furniture from the time period. There are two museum rooms and a visitor center where you can view a film of his life and browse the gift shop.

---

[62] https://www.nps.gov/thrb/index.htm

New York City, New York

Donald Trump
Family Home
Not open to the public
Trump Towers
725 Fifth Avenue
New York, New York 10022
Between East 56th and East 57th Streets

This private residence is not open to the public. However, the Trump Store, Trump Café, and Trump Grill are open to the public from 8:00 a.m. to 10:00 p.m.

Trump developed this one-hundred-million-dollar property that he completed in 1983. The décor is eighteenth-century French-style with an abundance of gold. The three-story penthouse on the sixty-sixth floor overlooks Central Park and Midtown Manhattan.

Oyster Bay, New York

Theodore Roosevelt
Family Home
Open to the public
Sagamore Hill
National Park Service[63]
20 Sagamore Hill Road
Oyster Bay, New York 11771

The visitor center and bookstore are open Wednesday through Sunday from 9:00 a.m. to 5:00 p.m. Tours of the home are offered from 10:00 a.m. to 4:00 p.m.

Begin your tour at the visitor center, then stroll the grounds and stop at the many kiosk markers along the path to learn about Theodore Roosevelt on your cell-phone audio tour. In the house, there is a guided tour given by the park's rangers. Ninety-nine percent of the original furniture and twelve thousand objects and personal items are available for viewing. Artifacts from Japan and Russia and animal mounts are on display as well as Roosevelt's hat and saber used in the Spanish-American War.

---

[63] https://www.nps.gov/sahi/index.htm

Oyster Bay, New York

Theodore Roosevelt
Final Resting Place
Open to the public
Youngs Memorial Cemetery[64]
134 Cove Road
Oyster Bay, New York 11771

Open daily from 9:00 a.m. until dusk.

Follow the same path as Roosevelt's funeral procession to the twenty-six steps that lead to the grave of the twenty-sixth president. In the quiet wooded section of the cemetery is a small granite headstone that marks the grave on a plot Roosevelt selected himself. Surrounded by an iron fence is the grave of Roosevelt and his wife, Edith.

---

[64] http://www.trgravesite.org/

Richmond Hill, New York

Donald Trump
Birthplace
Not open to the public
Jamaica Hospital Medical Center
8900 Van Wyck Expressway
Richmond Hill, Queens, New York 11418

Donald Trump was born on June 14, 1946, in this hospital in Queens. It is a working hospital and is not open to the public for tours.

Wilton, New York

Ulysses S. Grant
Grant Cottage
Open to the public
Ulysses S. Grant Cottage State Historic Site[65]
1000 Mount McGregor Road
Wilton, New York 12831

Open Memorial Day weekend through Labor Day on Wednesdays through Sundays from 10:00 a.m. to 4:00 p.m. Open Labor Day through Columbus Day on Saturdays and Sundays from 10:00 a.m. to 4:00 p.m. Open on Memorial Day, Labor Day, and Columbus Day.

Due to his illness, Grant's doctors suggested he go to the mountains so the clean air could soothe his throat cancer. He moved to his friend's Adirondack cottage on June 16, 1885, with his family, servants, and doctors so he could relax and complete his memoirs. He died here on July 23, 1885, just after finishing them. Tour the downstairs rooms to view original furniture, decorations, personal items, and the bed where he died. Stop at the visitor center to see an introductory film, exhibits, and displays. The gift shop has many books and memorabilia available for purchase.

---

[65] http://www.grantcottage.net/

NORTH CAROLINA

1. **Pineville, North Carolina**
   Birthplace: James Knox Polk

2. **Raleigh, North Carolina**
   Birthplace: Andrew Johnson

3. **Waxhaw, North Carolina**
   Birthplace: Andrew Jackson

Pineville, North Carolina

James Knox Polk
Birthplace
Open to the public
President James K. Polk Birthplace
North Carolina State Historic Site[66]
12031 Lancaster Highway
Pineville, North Carolina 28134

Open Tuesdays through Saturdays from 9:00 a.m. to 5:00 p.m. Closed on Sundays and Mondays.

James Knox Polk was born on November 2, 1795, in a log cabin on the family farm. He lived here for the first eleven years of his life. At the visitor center, you can view a film of Polk's life and explore a small museum with exhibits and memorabilia from Polk's childhood. There is a tour of the reconstructed log cabin, other small buildings, the grounds, and the gardens.

---

[66] http://www.jameskpolk.net/

Raleigh, North Carolina

Andrew Johnson
Birthplace
Open to the public
Original Site of Birth with Historic Marker:
123 Fayetteville Street
Raleigh, North Carolina 27601

Building Moved To:
Mordecai Historic Park
1 Mimosa Street
Raleigh, North Carolina 27604

The site is open Mondays, Wednesdays, Thursdays, Fridays, and Saturdays from 10:00 a.m. to 4:00 p.m. and on Sundays from 1:00 p.m. to 4:00 p.m.

Andrew Johnson was born on December 29, 1808, in the kitchen at the inn where his mother and father worked. The birthplace was moved from its original location several times to where it has now stood since 1976. The birthplace stands in Mordecai Historic Park near the North Carolina State Capitol. Visit the Johnson Birthplace, Mordecai House, and other buildings. There is a marker at the original site.

Waxhaw, North Carolina

Andrew Jackson
Birthplace
Open to the public
701 West South Main Street
Waxhaw, North Carolina 28173

Birthplace
Open to the public
Andrew Jackson State Park
196 Andrew Jackson Park Road
Lancaster, South Carolina 29720

Was he born in North Carolina or South Carolina? His birthplace is disputed to this day.[67] Each state claims to be the birthplace of Andrew Jackson. Historians in North Carolina believe Andrew Jackson was born in a log cabin on the Jackson family plantation in North Carolina. Jackson's father died in 1767, just before his birth. His father is buried in South Carolina, just south of the North Carolina border. It is believed that Jackson's mother stayed with her sister in South Carolina while visiting the grave of her husband. It is here, some say, that Andrew Jackson was born. It is unknown whether or not she made it home to North Carolina to give birth. There is a one-and-a-half-mile distance between the two sites, and there are markers and monuments at both claiming to be the birthplace of Andrew Jackson. So, was he born in North Carolina or South Carolina?

---

[67] https://www.nbcnews.com/id/wbna41936576#.V_JG55MrLBI

NORTH DAKOTA

1. **Medora, North Dakota**
   Presidential Library: Theodore Roosevelt

Medora, North Dakota

Theodore Roosevelt
Presidential Library
Opening in 2024
Theodore Roosevelt National Park[68]
Medora, North Dakota 58645

The Theodore Roosevelt Presidential Library will be an insight into the life and legacy of Theodore Roosevelt. The campus will include a research center and a state-of-the-art museum. Theodore Roosevelt spent many years ranching and living in the Badlands of North Dakota. There will be displays of Roosevelt's life from his childhood to his presidency to his life after his presidency. There will also be a recreation of the Elkhorn Ranch cabin he built, furnished as it would have been when he lived there. In the library, the photos and papers from the White House years will be fully digitalized. Check the website for updates on the completion of the Theodore Roosevelt Library.

---

[68] https://www.trlibrary.com/

OHIO

1. **Blooming Grove, Ohio**
   Birthplace: Warren G. Harding

2. **Canton, Ohio**
   Family Home: William McKinley
   First Ladies Museum: Ida Saxton McKinley
   Presidential Library and Museum: William McKinley
   Final Resting Place: William McKinley

3. **Cincinnati, Ohio**
   Birthplace: William Howard Taft

4. **Cleveland, Ohio**
   Final Resting Place: James Garfield

5. **Delaware, Ohio**
   Birthplace: Rutherford B. Hayes

6. **Fremont, Ohio**
   Family Home: Rutherford B. Hayes
   Presidential Library: Rutherford B. Hayes
   Final Resting Place: Rutherford B. Hayes

7. **Georgetown, Ohio**
   Boyhood Home: Ulysses S. Grant

8. **Marion, Ohio**
   Final Resting Place: Warren G. Harding
   Family Home: Warren G. Harding

9. **Mentor, Ohio**
   Family Home: James Garfield

10. **Moreland Hills, Ohio**
    Birthplace: James Garfield

11. **Niles, Ohio**
    Birthplace: William McKinley
    Birthplace Museum: William McKinley

12. **North Bend, Ohio**
    Final Resting Place: William Henry Harrison
    Birthplace: Benjamin Harrison

13. **Point Pleasant, Ohio**
    Birthplace: Ulysses S. Grant

14. **Poland, Ohio**
    Boyhood Home: William McKinley

Blooming Grove, Ohio

Warren G. Harding
Birthplace
Not open to the public
6297 Ohio Route 97
Blooming Grove, Ohio 44833

Warren G. Harding was born on November 2, 1865, in a small home on his family farm. The home no longer exists. There is a historic marker under a flag on the property of a private residence. It is not the original home and is not open to the public.

Canton, Ohio

Ida Saxton McKinley, William McKinley
First Ladies Museum, Family Home
Open to the public
Saxton McKinley House[69]
National Park Service
National First Ladies Library[70]
331 South Market Avenue
Canton, Ohio 44702

Tours are Tuesdays through Saturdays at 9:30 a.m., 10:30 a.m., 12:30 p.m., 1:30 p.m., and 2:30 p.m., plus on Sundays in June, July, and August at 12:30 p.m., 1:30 p.m., and 2:30 p.m. Closed on Mondays and holidays.

The home where McKinley and his wife, Ida, lived from 1878 until 1891 was actually the family home of Ida Saxton and her family. It was built in 1841 and has been restored to its Victorian style with wallpaper and furniture of the time. Docents dressed in period costumes lead tours through the elegant house that is actually dedicated to the First Ladies, and the third-floor ballroom is lined with their portraits. There are two buildings to visit: the Saxton McKinley House and the Education and Research Center on 205 Market Avenue South, where the guided tours begin.

---

[69] http://www.firstladies.org/SaxtonMcKinleyHouse.aspx
[70] https://www.nps.gov/fila/saxton-mckinley-house.htm

Canton, Ohio

William McKinley
Presidential Library and Museum
Open to the public
McKinley Presidential Library and Museum[71]
800 McKinley Monument Drive NW
Canton, Ohio 44708

Open Mondays through Fridays from 9:00 a.m.to 4:00 p.m. Closed on Easter, Memorial Day, Labor Day, Christmas, and New Year's Day.

A totally different experience than most Presidential Museums, your visit transports you to the past, the present, and into the future. There is so much to see, so plan to spend the whole day here. The McKinley Gallery in the Presidential Museum houses the largest collection of artifacts and records related to the life of McKinley. The museum also includes the Research Library and Archives, where records are available to the public. View the moon and stars, meteor showers, and constellations in the sixty-five-seat Hoover-Price Planetarium with presentations on the universe. Travel back to the days of the dinosaurs in Discover World, a hands-on science center with exhibits from the Mesozoic and Paleozoic eras, then move right into the displays on future science. Explore and learn in the Stark County Story; this exhibit brings you through two hundred years of artifacts showcasing the history of Stark County. Walk through and interact in the Street of Shops, a life-size replica of a historic town, and walk up the 108 steps to the McKinley Memorial, the final resting place of William McKinley. Finally, stop at the Museum Shoppe for a large selection of gifts and collectibles.

---

[71] http://mckinleymuseum.org/mckinley-memorial/

Canton, Ohio

William McKinley
Final Resting Place
Open to the public
William McKinley Tomb[72]
National Park Service
800 McKinley Monument Drive NW
Canton, Ohio 44708

Open Mondays through Saturdays from 9:00 a.m. to 4:00 p.m. and on Sundays from noon to 4:00 p.m. Closed on holidays.

The circular mausoleum topped with a pink granite dome stands at ninety-six feet tall and contains the bodies of William, his wife Ida, and their two daughters. The tomb is on a hillside overlooking the city of Canton, which McKinley called home.

---

[72] https://www.nps.gov/nr/travel/presidents/mckinley_tomb.html

Cincinnati, Ohio

William Howard Taft
Birthplace
Open to the public
William Howard Taft National Historic Site[73]
National Park Service
2038 Auburn Avenue
Cincinnati, Ohio 45219

Open seven days a week from 8:00 a.m. to 4:15 p.m. Closed on Thanksgiving, Christmas, and New Year's Day.

Shortly after the original structure was built in the 1840s, Taft's parents bought this Greek-Revival-style home. William Howard Taft was born on September 15, 1857, in the first-floor bedroom. Taft spent his childhood here until he left for Yale. In 1877, the house was damaged by fire and has since been restored with many improvements. The first floor has five rooms restored to the period, including the room where William Taft was born. It opened to the public in 1988. View a short film on the life of Taft in the Taft Education Center and Bookstore. A guided tour will show how the home looked during the time Taft lived here. There is also a historic marker in front.

[73] https://www.nps.gov/wiho/index.htm

Cleveland, Ohio

James Garfield
Final Resting Place
Open to the public
Lake View Cemetery[74]
12316 Euclid Avenue
Cleveland, Ohio 44106

The cemetery is open daily from 7:30 a.m. to 5:30 p.m. The tomb is open April through November from 9:00 a.m. to 4:00 p.m.

James Garfield was shot on July 2, 1881, and was severely injured. He died on September 19, 1881, at only forty-nine years old. The Garfield Monument stands at 180 feet tall and is one of the largest presidential tombs. On the outside, there are terracotta panels depicting the life of Garfield. Inside, there are mosaics, stained glass windows, red granite columns, and a statue of James Garfield. The stairs lead to the outside balcony. The casket of President James Garfield is draped with an American flag. Next to him is his wife's casket.

---

[74] http://lakeviewcemetery.com/visit/points-of-interest/james-a-garfield-memorial/

Delaware, Ohio

Rutherford B. Hayes
Birthplace
Open to the public
Rutherford B. Hayes Birthplace
17 East William Street
Delaware, Ohio 43015

Rutherford B. Hayes was born on October 4, 1817, in the two-story brick home built by his father. His father passed away just three months before his birth, and he only lived in the home for a very short time, which was lost in a fire in 1910. A gas station is now at the site of the birthplace. A new statue of Rutherford B. Hayes stands on the corner of Sandusky and William Streets to honor the former president.

Fremont, Ohio

Rutherford B. Hayes
Family Home
Open to the public
Rutherford B. Hayes Presidential Center[75]
Spiegel Grove
1337 Hayes Avenue
Fremont, Ohio 43420

This home at Spiegel Grove is located on the twenty-five-acre grounds of the Rutherford B. Hayes Presidential Center and is open Mondays through Saturdays from 9:00 a.m. to 5:00 p.m. Closed on Sundays. Closed on Mondays in January, February, and March.

Hayes moved into this eight-bedroom, thirty-one-room mansion in 1873. Over the years, he made many changes and additions to the home. Six rooms were restored in 2011 with many of the original furnishings and decorations. Rutherford and Lucy returned to live here following his presidency. Hayes particularly enjoyed the wrap-around veranda where he spent most of his time.

---

[75] http://www.rbhayes.org/

Fremont, Ohio

Rutherford B. Hayes
Presidential Library and Museum
Open to the public
Rutherford B. Hayes Presidential Center[76]
Spiegel Grove
1337 Hayes Avenue
Fremont, Ohio 43420

The Rutherford B. Hayes Presidential Center is located on the grounds of Spiegel Grove. It is open Mondays through Saturdays from 9:00 a.m. to 5:00 p.m. Closed on Sundays. Closed on Mondays in January, February, and March.

America's first privately owned presidential library was opened in 1916 by the family to preserve the twelve-thousand-volume book collection of Hayes. The museum, renovated in 2016, houses artifacts from the life of Hayes, including articles from his military career, his Civil War service, and his time as president.

---

[76] http://www.rbhayes.org/

Fremont, Ohio

Rutherford B. Hayes
Final Resting Place
Open to the public
Rutherford B. Hayes Presidential Center[77]
Spiegel Grove
1337 Hayes Avenue
Fremont, Ohio 43420

The grave is located on the grounds of the Rutherford B. Hayes Presidential Center on Spiegel Grove and is open to the public Mondays through Saturdays from 9:00 a.m. to 5:00 p.m. Closed on Sundays. Closed on Mondays in January, February, and March.

Rutherford B. Hayes died on January 17, 1893. He was first buried with his wife in Oakwood Cemetery, a public cemetery in his town. Hayes and his wife were reinterred in 1916 on the grounds of the Presidential Center in the Hayes Tomb, which is located on their favorite spot in Spiegel Grove.

---

[77] http://www.rbhayes.org/

Georgetown, Ohio

Ulysses S. Grant
Boyhood Home
Open to the public
Ulysses S. Grant Boyhood Home[78]
219 East Grant Avenue
Georgetown, Ohio 45121

Open from May 1 to October 31 on Wednesdays through Sundays from noon until 5:00 p.m. Closed on Mondays and Tuesdays.

This home, the two-room schoolhouse, and the tannery of the eighteenth president are all open for tours. Grant lived here from the age of one until he left for West Point in 1839. The home was built in 1823, and the schoolhouse was built in 1829. The house is decorated with period pieces as well as some of the original furnishings.

---

[78] usgrantboyhoodhome.org

Marion, Ohio

Warren G. Harding
Family Home
Open to the public
President Harding Home and Museum[79]
Ohio Historical Society
380 Mount Vernon Avenue
Marion, Ohio 43302

Open Memorial Day through Labor Day on Wednesdays through Saturdays from 9:30 a.m. to 5:00 p.m. Open in September and October on Saturdays from 9:30 a.m. to 5:00 p.m. and on Sundays from noon until 5:00 p.m.

This Queen-Anne-style home was built in 1890 by Warren and his wife Florence the year before they were married. They lived here until they moved into the White House in 1921. Harding died while serving as president, and the home was turned into a museum after the death of his wife fifteen months later. The home has almost all of the original furniture and has been restored to the period when President Harding lived here. In addition to the home, visit the new Warren G. Harding Presidential Library and Museum structure, which resembles the White House, just completed in 2021. The building contains an exhibit gallery, presidential artifacts and documents, a gift shop, and an event space.

---

[79] http://www.hardinghome.org/

Marion, Ohio

Warren G. Harding
Final Resting Place
Open to the public
Harding Tomb[80]
Warren Harding Memorial Park
966-870 Delaware Avenue
Marion, Ohio 43302

Warren Harding died on August 2, 1923, while on a trip during his presidency. He was originally buried in a receiving vault in the Marion County Cemetery at 620 Delaware Avenue. He was reinterred to his final resting place in 1927. The circular monument of white Georgian marble is designed like a round Greek temple with an open court. There are two black granite headstones for Harding and his wife, Florence.

---

[80] http://www.hardinghome.org/harding-memorial/

Mentor, Ohio

James Garfield
Family Home
Open to the public
Lawnfield
James A. Garfield National Historic Site[81]
National Park Service
8095 Mentor Avenue
Mentor, Ohio 44060

Open May through October on Mondays through Saturdays from 10:00 a.m. to 5:00 p.m. and on Sundays from noon until 5:00 p.m. Open November through April for the same hours on Fridays, Saturdays, and Sundays only. Closed on holidays.

Garfield and his wife Lucretia bought this old farmhouse and 120 acres of land in 1876. Over the next few years, they renovated, building an addition, a third floor, and a huge front porch. The back-room addition became his campaign office, and the porch became famous for his "front porch campaign." After Garfield's death, Lucretia stayed and added a fireproof "memory room" memorial and library wing to save his papers and personal memorabilia. The house has been restored with 1880s decor. The visitor center has displays about Garfield's life.

---

[81] https://www.nps.gov/jaga/index.htm

Moreland Hills, Ohio

James Garfield
Open to the public
James A. Garfield Memorial Cabin
Village of Moreland Hills
4350 S.O.M. Center Road
Moreland Hills, Ohio 44022

Open June through September on Saturdays from 10:00 a.m. to 1:00 p.m.

James Garfield was born in a small log cabin on November 19, 1831. Garfield's father built the original log cabin in 1830, though it was destroyed by a fire. The replica is furnished very simply, as it would have been in Garfield's early days. There is a trail that leads to the location of the original cabin.

Niles, Ohio

William McKinley
Birthplace
Open to the public
The National McKinley Birthplace Museum[82]
36 South Main Street
Niles, Ohio 44446

Open Mondays through Wednesdays from 9:00 a.m. to 5:00 p.m. and on Thursdays from 9:00 a.m. to 3:00 p.m. Closed on Fridays, Saturdays, and Sundays. Be sure to call for more information.

William McKinley was born here on January 29, 1843. The historical marker in front of the birthplace states that the house was moved from the original site, which had been destroyed by a fire in 1937. The site was chosen because McKinley had attended a one-room schoolhouse that had been at this location. The replica, albeit slightly larger than the original, was built in 2002. The Birthplace Memorial is at 40 South Main Street, one block north of the original site.

---

[82] https://mckinleybirthplacemuseum.org/

Niles, Ohio

William McKinley
Birthplace Memorial
Open to the public
The National McKinley Birthplace Memorial and Museum[83]
40 South Main Street
Niles, Ohio 44446

Open Mondays through Wednesdays from 9:00 a.m. to 5:00 p.m. and on Thursdays from 9:00 a.m. to 3:00 p.m. Closed on Fridays, Saturdays, and Sundays.

The Birthplace Museum has a timeline of McKinley's personal life, his time in war and government, his campaign trail, and his assassination. There is a collection of memorabilia from the Civil War and the Spanish-American War. It showcases many of the McKinleys's personal furnishings as well. Self-guided and guided tours are available. The knowledgeable staff is very eager to share facts and stories of McKinley's life.

---

[83] https://mckinleybirthplacemuseum.org/

North Bend, Ohio

William Henry Harrison
Final Resting Place
Open to the public
William Henry Harrison Tomb
41 Cliff Road
North Bend, Ohio 45052

The site is open year-round during daylight hours. The tomb gate is open from March 2 until December 14 from 10:00 a.m. to 6 p.m. daily.

Harrison had been in office for thirty-one days when he died of pneumonia on April 4, 1841. His wife, Anna, had not yet moved into the White House. Because of his unexpected death, the plot he had chosen for his final resting place on Mount Nebo was not yet ready, so he was temporarily laid to rest in the Congressional Cemetery in Washington D.C. On July 7, 1841, Harrison's body was moved to the vault on the spot he had chosen for his final resting place overlooking the Ohio River in North Bend. The grave is marked with a one-hundred-foot monument. Anna and other family members are also in the vaults in the tomb.

North Bend, Ohio

Benjamin Harrison
Birthplace
Not open to the public
Benjamin Harrison Birthplace
Corner of Symmes and Washington Streets
North Bend, Ohio 45052

Benjamin Harrison was born on August 24, 1833, on a six-hundred-acre family farm that belonged to his grandfather, William Henry Harrison. There is a historical marker on the corner where the house once stood. The home on the property is not the original and is a private residence, which is not open to the public.

Point Pleasant, Ohio

Hiram Ulysses Grant
Birthplace
Open to the public
Grant's Birthplace State Memorial[84]
1551 OH-232
Point Pleasant, Ohio 45153

The home is open from April through October 15 on Wednesdays through Saturdays from 9:30 a.m. to noon and 1:00 p.m. to 5:00 p.m. Open on Sundays from 1:00 p.m. to 5:00 p.m.

Ulysses S. Grant, named Hiram Ulysses Grant, was born on April 27, 1822, in a little one-room cabin built in 1817. The Grant family only lived here for a very short time. Docents tell the story of how the cabin was moved onto a barge in 1890 and traveled up and down the river before being put on a train so people could view the home of a president. The house was returned to its original location in 1927. The restored, now three-room cabin has period-style furnishings and some items that belonged to Grant. There is a historic marker on the site.

---

[84] https://www.ohiohistory.org/visit/museum-and-site-locator/us-grant-birthplace

Poland, Ohio

William McKinley
Boyhood Home
Not open to the public
William McKinley Boyhood Home Historic Marker
202 South Main Street
Poland, Ohio 44514

Boyhood School
Poland Academy Historic Marker
50 College Street
Poland, Ohio 44514

In 1852, when McKinley was nine, his family moved to Poland, Ohio, so that the children could receive a quality education. William attended the elite Poland Academy until he graduated high school. There are markers at the location of both the home and the school.

OREGON

1. **Newberg, Oregon**
   Childhood Home: Herbert Hoover

Newberg, Oregon

Herbert Hoover
Childhood Home
Open to the public
Herbert Hoover-Minthorn House Museum[85]
115 South River Street
Newberg, Oregon 97132

Open from March through November on Wednesdays through Sundays from 1:00 p.m. to 4:00 p.m.

Herbert Hoover was born on August 10, 1874, in West Branch, Iowa. Sadly, his father died when he was six, and his mother died when he was nine. He, his sister, and his brother were separated from one another and sent away to live with relatives. Herbert, who was called "Bertie," was sent to Oregon to live with his uncle, a Quaker physician. This house is the oldest house in Newberg and was built in 1881. Tour the home to see the actual bedroom furniture, rocking chairs, and other furnishings collected by the family.

---

[85] http://hooverminthorn.org/home/

PENNSYLVANIA

1. **Gettysburg, Pennsylvania**
   Retirement Home: Dwight D. Eisenhower

2. **Lancaster, Pennsylvania**
   Family Home: James Buchanan
   Final Resting Place: James Buchanan

3. **Mercersburg, Pennsylvania**
   Birthplace: James Buchanan
   Birthplace Relocated Cabin: James Buchanan
   Childhood Home: James Buchanan

4. **Scranton, Pennsylvania**
   Birthplace: Joseph Biden
   Childhood Home: Joseph Biden

Gettysburg, Pennsylvania

Dwight D. Eisenhower
Retirement Home
Open to the public
National Park Service
Eisenhower National Historic Site
Gettysburg National Military Park, Museum, and Visitor Center[86]
1195 Baltimore Pike
Gettysburg, Pennsylvania 17325

Tours depart daily from the Gettysburg National Military Park, Museum, and Visitor Center. Museum and Visitor Center hours are April through October from 8:00 a.m. to 6:00 p.m. and November through March from 9:00 a.m. to 5:00 p.m. Closed on Thanksgiving, Christmas, and New Year's Day. There is so much to do here, so plan to spend more than a day. The visitor center alone is a tourist destination.

All tours start at the Gettysburg National Military Park, Museum, and Visitor Center. The visitor center is enormous, with films, museums, interactive exhibits, and a cyclorama all centered on the American Civil War and Lincoln's Gettysburg Address. There are several Civil War battlefield tours and a tour of the Eisenhower House and Farm. Shuttle busses take the tour group to the sites. Once you arrive, you are welcome to spend as much time as needed at the site. Busses depart hourly to bring you back to the visitor center.

Ike and Mamie Eisenhower bought the run-down farmhouse to restore and retire to in 1951. The farmhouse on the 189-acre farm dates back to the early 1700s. During reconstruction, some of the original house was salvaged and used. The farmhouse is the only house Eisenhower ever owned and has 98 percent of the original furnishings, including the dining room furniture Mamie bought in 1927 that traveled to many homes with her. The living room contains several presidential gifts and collections. See Ike's sunroom, where he enjoyed painting

---

[86] http://www.gettysburgfoundation.org/

during his retirement, and see the 1950s-style kitchen. Your visit includes a self-guided tour of the twenty-four-room farmhouse, the guesthouse, and the barns. The reception center has a video, exhibits, and a bookstore.

Lancaster, Pennsylvania

James Buchanan
Family Home
Open to the public
Wheatland
LancasterHistory[87]
230 North President Avenue
Lancaster, Pennsylvania 17603

Wheatland is open Mondays through Saturdays from 10:00 a.m. to 5:00 p.m. Closed on Sundays. Closed on Thanksgiving, Christmas Eve, and Christmas Day, and from December 31 through January 8. All tours start in the visitor center, where you can view a short film and visit the museum and gift shop.

This brick-style home was built in 1828 on the beautiful wheat fields. President Buchanan named his beloved home Wheatland. You can explore the house with a tour given by knowledgeable guides dressed in traditional period clothing. Experience the history of the home, the grounds, the library, the exhibit gallery, and the bookstore.

---

[87] https://www.lancasterhistory.org/visit/wheatland

Lancaster, Pennsylvania

James Buchanan
Final Resting Place
Open to the public
Woodward Hill Cemetery[88]
Buchanan Tomb
501 South Queen Street
Lancaster, Pennsylvania 17603

Open May through October from 7:00 a.m. to 6:00 p.m. and November through April from 7:00 a.m. to 5:00 p.m.

James Buchanan died on June 1, 1868, at his Wheatland home. He is buried in a cemetery a short distance from Wheatland in a plot he chose because of the view of Lancaster. Follow the signs to his grave located on the top of a hill marked by an American flag.

---

[88] http://www.woodwardhillcemetery.com

Mercersburg, Pennsylvania

James Buchanan
Birthplace
Open to the public
Buchanan Birthplace State Park
2831 Stony Batter Road
Mercersburg, Pennsylvania 17236

The park is open daily, and the office is open Mondays through Saturdays from 7:00 a.m. to 5:00 p.m.

This is another "off the beaten path" location. The park is in Mercersburg, Pennsylvania, near the village of Cove Gap along PA 16. From US 30 at Fort Loudon, take PA 75 south and follow signs to Cove Gap and the park. To me, this was a most breathtaking sight, deep in the woods during the early morning of a cold fall day. Buchanan's father bought Tom's Trading Place and the surrounding farm in 1789 and renamed it Stony Batter after his ancestor's home in Northern Ireland. James Buchanan was born here in a little log cabin on April 23, 1791. They lived here for six more years while his father worked in the stables and the store until his father sold it in 1796. There is a thirty-one-foot-tall stone pyramid to mark the spot where the birthplace cabin stood. The relocated cabin is located on the grounds of the nearby Mercersburg Academy.

Mercersburg, Pennsylvania

James Buchanan
Birthplace
Open to the public
Buchanan Birthplace Relocated Cabin
Mercersburg Academy
300 East Seminary Street
Mercersburg, Pennsylvania 17236

The cabin can be viewed during daylight hours on the grounds of Mercersburg Academy. It is very difficult to find—I had to ask students to direct me. It is under the trees behind the ball field, literally "out in left field."

Mercersburg, Pennsylvania

James Buchanan
Childhood Home
Not open to the public
Buchanan Childhood Home
17 North Main Street
Mercersburg, Pennsylvania 17236

Buchanan's father built this home in 1796. The family moved into the house and stayed there throughout James Buchanan's childhood. The house is now a private residence and is not open to the public, but there is a historical marker by the road.

Scranton, Pennsylvania

Joseph Biden
Birthplace
Not open to the public
930 Hickory Street
Scranton, Pennsylvania 18505

Joseph Robinette Biden Jr. was born on November 20, 1942, at St. Mary's Hospital. Biden was born and raised in Scranton. The former hospital has closed, and the building now houses the Yeshiva Beth Moshe School, which is not open to the public.

Scranton, Pennsylvania

Joseph Biden
Childhood Home
Not open to the public
2446 North Washington Avenue
Scranton, Pennsylvania 18509

Joe Biden spent his childhood in Scranton. On election day, November 3, 2020, he returned to the neighborhood where he grew up. When he stopped at his childhood home, he wrote on the wall, "From this house to the White House with the Grace of God." The home is a private residence and is not open to the public.

RHODE ISLAND

1. **Newport, Rhode Island**
   Summer White House: John F. Kennedy
   Summer White House: Dwight D. Eisenhower
   St. Mary's Roman Catholic Church: John F. Kennedy

Newport, Rhode Island

John F. Kennedy
Summer White House
Not open to the public
Hammersmith Farm
225 Harrison Avenue
Newport, Rhode Island 02840

Built for John W. Auchincloss in 1887, this Victorian mansion was used for the wedding reception of John F. Kennedy and Jacqueline Bouvier in 1953. It became the unofficial Summer White House during the Kennedy presidency. It is not open to the public, but it is worth the visit to beautiful Newport, Rhode Island. Take a boat tour of Newport to view the house.

Susan Alba

Newport, Rhode Island

John F. Kennedy
St. Mary's Roman Catholic Church
Open to the public
St. Mary's Church
12 William Street
Newport, Rhode Island 02840

Kennedy married Jacqueline Bouvier in this Newport church on September 12, 1953. St. Mary's Church is the oldest Roman Catholic parish in Rhode Island. It has been recently renovated, and you can still see the seat that the Kennedys used. I mentioned this church because of its location in beautiful Newport. The historical marker reads:

St. Mary's Parish
was founded April 8, 1828, and is the
oldest Parish in the Diocese of Providence.
Present structure begun August 7, 1848.
Dedicated on August 15, 1884.
President John F. Kennedy
and Jacqueline Lee Bouvier
were married here on
September 12, 1953.
St. Mary's was designated
A National Historic Shrine
November 24, 1968.

204

Newport, Rhode Island

Dwight D. Eisenhower
Summer White House
Open to the public
Eisenhower House[89]
Fort Adams State Park
1 Lincoln Drive
Newport, Rhode Island 02840

---

[89] http://www.eisenhowerhouse.com

Open from Memorial Day until Labor Day on Mondays from 10:00 a.m. to 2:00 p.m. It is in Fort Adams State Park and is accessible to view and walk the grounds every day throughout the year.

The Eisenhower House, a stately mansion in Fort Adams State Park, was erected in 1873. Eisenhower spent summers here from 1957 to 1960. He said, "The White House is wherever the president happens to be." The historic home is now used for functions such as weddings, with its breathtaking views of Narragansett Bay and Newport Harbor. It is worth the visit to Fort Adams State Park to learn of the history here in Newport, Rhode Island.

SOUTH CAROLINA

1. **Columbia, South Carolina**
   Childhood Home: Thomas Woodrow Wilson

2. **Lancaster, South Carolina**
   Birthplace State Park: Andrew Jackson

Columbia, South Carolina

Thomas Woodrow Wilson
Childhood Home
Open to the public
Woodrow Wilson Family Home[90]
1705 Hampton Street
Columbia, South Carolina 29201

Open Tuesdays through Saturdays. Tours are at 11:30 a.m. and 2:30 p.m. and on Sundays at 2:30 p.m. All tours start at the Gift Shop at Robert Mills at 1616 Blanding Street. Tours of other homes are also available.

This Victorian cottage that the Wilsons lived in from 1870 until 1874 is the only home ever owned by the family. It has been scientifically restored to the way it was in the 1870s. There is also the kitchen house, privy, and carriage house to view on the property. Visit the gardens with a formal front yard and a working backyard with vegetable and flower beds as planned by the future president's mother, Jessie.

---

[90] http://www.historiccolumbia.org/woodrow-wilson-family-home

Lancaster, South Carolina

Andrew Jackson
Birthplace
Open to the public
Andrew Jackson State Park
196 Andrew Jackson Park Road
Lancaster, South Carolina 29720
End of Route 1105 on East Rebound Road

Birthplace
Open to the public
701 West South Main Street
Waxhaw, North Carolina 28173

This entry may sound familiar, but I feel it bears repeating. The actual location of the birthplace of Andrew Jackson has never been verified. As stated before, both North Carolina and South Carolina claim to be the birthplace due to the circumstances.

Was Jackson born in North Carolina or South Carolina? The birthplace is disputed to this day. Each state claims to be the birthplace of Andrew Jackson. Historians in North Carolina believe that Andrew Jackson was born in the log cabin on the Jackson family plantation in North Carolina. Jackson's father died in 1767, just before his birth. His father is buried in South Carolina, just south of the North Carolina border. It is believed that Jackson's mother stayed with her sister in South Carolina while visiting the grave of her husband. It is here, some say, that Andrew Jackson was born. It is unknown whether she made it home to North Carolina to give birth. There is a one-and-one-half-mile distance between the two sites. There are markers and monuments in both sites claiming to be the birthplace of Andrew Jackson. So, was he born in North Carolina or South Carolina?

TENNESSEE

1. **Columbia, Tennessee**
   Family Home: James K. Polk

2. **Greeneville, Tennessee**
   Presidential Library and Museum: Andrew Johnson
   Family Home: Andrew Johnson
   Final Resting Place: Andrew Johnson

3. **Harrogate, Tennessee**
   Presidential Museum: Abraham Lincoln

4. **Hermitage, Tennessee**
   Family Home: Andrew Jackson
   Final Resting Place: Andrew Jackson

5. **Nashville, Tennessee**
   Final Resting Place: James K. Polk
   Family Home: James K. Polk

Columbia, Tennessee

James K. Polk
Family Home
Open to the public
President James K. Polk Home and Museum[91]
301 West 7th Street
Columbia, Tennessee 38401

April through October, the home is open Mondays through Saturdays from 9:00 a.m. to 5:00 p.m. and on Sundays from 1:00 p.m. to 5:00 p.m. From November through March, the home is open Mondays through Saturdays from 9:00 a.m. to 4:00 p.m. and on Sundays from 1:00 p.m. to 5:00 p.m. Closed on Thanksgiving, Christmas Eve, Christmas Day, and New Year's Day.

The father of James K. Polk built this Federal-style house, typical of Tennessee architecture, in 1816. James K. Polk lived in this family home with his parents until his marriage in 1824. Much of the furnishings, clothing, and paintings are from Polk Place, the home of James and his wife, Sarah. There is a tour of the main house, and across the street is a visitor center, which was once the home of Sarah's sister. Visit the exhibition in the hall, and enjoy the gardens. Start your tour and view a film at the visitor center.

[91] http://www.jameskpolk.com/

Greeneville, Tennessee

Andrew Johnson
Presidential Library and Museum
Open to the public
Andrew Johnson National Historic Site
National Park Service
101 North College Street
Greeneville, Tennessee 37743

Open Mondays through Fridays from 9:00 a.m. to 5:00 p.m. You are advised to call first.

This small library and museum is located on the campus of Tusculum University in the oldest building on campus. The museum houses furnishings and personal effects of Andrew Johnson. The exhibits include displays about the Civil War times and items from his family life.

Greeneville, Tennessee

Andrew Johnson
Family Home
Open to the public
Andrew Johnson National Historic Site[92]
National Park Service
101 North College Street
Greeneville, Tennessee 37743

Open daily from 9:00 a.m. to 5:00 p.m. Closed on Thanksgiving, Christmas, and New Year's Day.

This home was used to house Confederate soldiers by Johnson during the Civil War. Begin your tour at the visitor center, where you can view a short film. There are four parts of the tour: the tailor shop and museum with many artifacts and memorabilia; the early home where Johnson lived when he was a tailor, with original furnishings and artifacts; the homestead Johnson owned before and after his presidency; and the cemetery.

---

[92] https://www.nps.gov/anjo/index.htm

Greeneville, Tennessee

Andrew Johnson
Final Resting Place
Open to the public
Andrew Johnson National Cemetery[93]
National Park Service
121 Monument Avenue
Greeneville, Tennessee 37743

Open daily from 9:00 a.m. to 5:00 p.m. Closed on Thanksgiving, Christmas, and New Year's Day.

Andrew Johnson bought this land in 1852 and requested it as his final resting place. The tall obelisk over his grave, also known as Monument Hill, was built in 1878. Jackson and his wife are buried here along with their children and many other family members.

---

[93] https://www.nps.gov/anjo/cemeteryhist.htm

Harrogate, Tennessee

Abraham Lincoln
Presidential Library and Museum
Open to the public
Abraham Lincoln Library and Museum
120 Mars-Debusk Parkway
Harrogate, Tennessee 37752

Open weekdays from 10:00 a.m. to 5:00 p.m., on Saturdays from noon to 5:00 p.m., and on Sundays from 1:00 p.m. to 5:00 p.m.

Located on the Lincoln Memorial University campus, this beautiful two-story museum houses many Civil War artifacts as well as several of Lincoln's personal items. A timeline of events takes you through Lincoln's life, his night at Ford's Theater, and his funeral. On display is the cane Lincoln used in Ford's Theater on the night he was shot. This museum was funded by a very generous donation from Colonel Harland Sanders, founder of Kentucky Fried Chicken. The original KFC is less than an hour away in Kentucky.

Hermitage, Tennessee

Andrew Jackson
Family Home
Open to the public
The Hermitage[94]
4580 Rachel's Lane
Hermitage, Tennessee 37076

Open every day except Thanksgiving and Christmas. Open from October 16 to March 14 from 9:00 a.m. to 5:00 p.m. and from March 15 to October 15 from 8:30 a.m. to 5:00 p.m.

Jackson built his original home on the 625-acre estate in 1821. The home was later destroyed by a fire. After purchasing more land, he rebuilt the Greek-Revival-style home on the now one-thousand-acre plantation. The mansion has been restored and has many of Jackson's personal belongings, reflecting life in the 1830s and 1840s. See the original home, standing twenty-four by twenty-six feet and one-and-one-half stories; Jackson converted it into the slave quarters. Stroll the beautiful Hermitage grounds with over thirty signs to interpret Jackson's life. Start at the visitor center, tour the home, view a film in the theater, and visit the gift shop.

---

[94] http://thehermitage.com

Hermitage, Tennessee

Andrew Jackson
Final Resting Place
Open to the public
The Hermitage[95]
4580 Rachel's Lane
Hermitage, Tennessee 37076

Open every day except on Thanksgiving and Christmas. Open from October 16 to March 14 from 9:00 a.m. to 5:00 p.m. and from March 15 to October 15 from 8:30 a.m. to 5:00 p.m.

The Hermitage tulip gardens are the center of the grounds. Andrew Jackson and his wife, Rachel, are buried on this site under the cupola. Jackson's Tomb is simply inscribed:

General Andrew Jackson
March 15, 1767
June 8, 1845

---

[95] http://thehermitage.com/

Nashville, Tennessee

James K. Polk
Final Resting Place
Open to the public
Tennessee State Capitol, President James K. Polk Tomb[96]
600 Dr. Martin L King, Jr. Boulevard
Nashville, Tennessee 37243

The grave on the grounds of the Tennessee State Capitol is open to the public at all times.

James K. Polk died on June 15, 1849, just three months after leaving the office of the presidency. He was originally buried in the Nashville City Cemetery. His body was then moved to Polk Place, the home where he died. Polk's wife, Sarah, died forty-two years after his death, and she was buried beside her husband at Polk Place. On September 19, 1893, Polk and his wife were moved again to their final resting place at the Tennessee State Capitol.

---

[96] https://https://www.atlasobscura.com/places/james-k-polk-tomb

Nashville, Tennessee

James K. Polk
Family Home
Not open to the public
Polk Place
211 7th Avenue North
Nashville, Tennessee 37219

Polk Place was the home of James and Sarah Polk. It was his final residence and where he died on June 15, 1849. Sarah stayed in the home until her death in 1891. The house no longer exists, but there is a marker at the place where the home stood. The furnishings from Polk Place are now on exhibit at the President James K. Polk Home and Museum in Columbia, Tennessee.

TEXAS

1. **Austin, Texas**
   Presidential Library and Museum: Lyndon Baines Johnson

2. **College Station, Texas**
   Presidential Library and Museum: George H. W. Bush
   Final Resting Place: George H. W. Bush

3. **Dallas, Texas**
   Presidential Library and Museum: George W. Bush
   The Sixth-Floor Museum at Dealey Plaza: John F. Kennedy

4. **Denison, Texas**
   Birthplace: Dwight D. Eisenhower

5. **Johnson City, Texas**
   National Historical Park: Lyndon Baines Johnson
   Childhood Home: Lyndon Baines Johnson

6. **Midland, Texas**
   Childhood Home: George W. Bush

7. **Stonewall, Texas**
   Birthplace: Lyndon Baines Johnson
   Texas White House: Lyndon Baines Johnson
   Final Resting Place: Lyndon Baines Johnson

Austin, Texas

Lyndon Baines Johnson
Presidential Library and Museum
Open to the public
Lyndon Baines Johnson Library and Museum[97]
Administered by the National Archives and Records Administration
University of Texas at Austin
2313 Red River Street
Austin, Texas 78705

Open daily from 9:00 a.m. to 5:00 p.m. Closed on Thanksgiving, Christmas, and New Year's Day.

Located on a thirty-acre site at the University of Texas at Austin, this impressive ten-story Presidential Library and Museum houses forty-five million documents and 650,000 photos. Enter the lobby on Level 3 and see the limousine that President Johnson used in Texas after his presidency. View a film on the life of LBJ, and continue to a very well-done timeline on the life of the Johnson family to hear hundreds of recordings and stories. The impressive center marble staircase takes you to the Great Hall on Level 4, where you can see into the four floors of glass-enclosed library rooms containing forty-five million pages of documents in the LBJ Library Archives. There are interactive exhibits and artifacts, and you can view murals and paintings of all of the presidents and their wives. See exhibits including The Assassination of President John F. Kennedy. Continue to Level 10 and learn about the personal life of LBJ, his Texas ranch, and his life in the White House as you step into a replica of the Oval Office as it was during the LBJ presidency. The gift shop offers many unique items honoring President Johnson. This is an excellent, extremely educational experience for learning about LBJ.

---

[97] http://www.lbjlibrary.org/

College Station, Texas

George H. W. Bush
Presidential Library and Museum
Open to the public
George H. W. Bush Presidential Library and Museum[98]
Administered by the National Archives and Records Administration
Texas A&M University
1000 George Bush Drive West
College Station, Texas 77845

Open Mondays through Saturdays from 9:30 a.m. to 5:00 p.m. and on Sundays from noon until 5:00 p.m. Closed on Thanksgiving, Christmas, and New Year's Day.

The library and museum are on the campus of Texas A&M University. The library holds a large collection of over thirty-five million pages of official papers and photos from Bush's presidency. The museum has memorabilia from Bush's early life to the present time. On display are pictures from his childhood, a model of the airplane he flew in WWII, the wedding dress worn by Barbara Bush, a small replica of the Oval Office, a piece of the Berlin Wall, his boat from his Kennebunkport residence, his Secret Service car, statues, and many videos of his life.

---

[98] https://bush41.org/

Susan Alba

College Station, Texas

George H. W. Bush
Final Resting Place
Open to the public
George H. W. Bush Presidential Library and Museum
Texas A&M University
1000 George Bush Drive West
College Station, Texas 77845

The site chosen and designed by George and Barbara Bush is just a short walk from the museum through the flower gardens. Walk the path that leads to the secluded reflecting pool and over the bridge crossing into the gates of the gravesite. Visit the grave of George and Barbara along with their young daughter Robin, who is also buried here.

Dallas, Texas

John F. Kennedy
The Sixth Floor Museum at Dealey Plaza
Open to the public
The Sixth-Floor Museum at Dealey Plaza[99]
411 Elm Street
Dallas, Texas 75202

Open daily on Mondays from noon to 6:00 p.m. and on Tuesdays through Sundays from 10:00 a.m. to 6:00 p.m. (last ticket sold at 5:15 p.m.). Closed on Thanksgiving and Christmas. Check website for holiday hours.

JFK and the Memory of a Nation chronicles the events and aftermath of the assassination of President Kennedy on November 22, 1963. Follow the timeline of events, and see historical images, artifacts, and news footage. Exhibits include The Early Sixties, The Trip to Texas, The Corner Window, Crisis Hours, and many more leading up to The Legacy of JFK. Stop in at the visitor center and the café across the street.

A short drive from the museum is the Hilton Fort Worth, where Kennedy spent his last night. At the entrance, there is a statue and memorial display with photos and the story of what occurred in Dallas.

---

[99] www.jfk.org

Dallas, Texas

George W. Bush
Presidential Library and Museum
Open to the public
George W. Bush Presidential Library and Museum[100]
Administered by the National Archives and Records Administration
Southern Methodist University
2943 SMU Boulevard
Dallas, Texas 75205

Open Mondays through Saturdays from 9:00 a.m. to 5:00 p.m. and on Sundays from noon to 5:00 p.m.

This museum houses a very moving memorial to the events of September 11, 2001, honoring those who lost their lives at the World Trade Center. Artifacts include steel from the World Trade Center and the bullhorn the president used. There is a replica of the Presidential Oval Office, photos, videos, and more. Much of the museum is dedicated to Bush's love for his family. Visit Café 43, a full-service restaurant inside the Presidential Library, or the Courtyard Café. There is also a museum store.

---

[100] http://www.georgewbushlibrary.smu.edu/

Denison, Texas

Dwight D. Eisenhower
Birthplace
Open to the public
Eisenhower Birthplace State Historic Site[101]
609 South Lamar Avenue
Denison, Texas 75021

Open Tuesdays through Saturdays from 9:00 a.m. to 5:00 p.m. and on Sundays from 1:00 p.m. to 5:00 p.m. Last tour begins at 4:00 p.m. Closed on Thanksgiving, Christmas Eve, Christmas Day, New Year's Eve, and New Year's Day.

Dwight David Eisenhower was born on October 14, 1890, in the downstairs bedroom of the two-story home in this ten-acre park. Tours begin with a video in the visitor center. Take the thirty-minute guided tour of the birthplace. The home is furnished much as it was in the 1890s. You can look into all the rooms, including the bedroom where Eisenhower was born. Visit Ike's statue on the beautifully manicured grounds.

---

[101] http://www.thc.texas.gov/historic-sites/eisenhower-birthplace-state-historic-site

Johnson City, Texas

Lyndon B. Johnson
National Historical Park
Open to the public
Lyndon B. Johnson National Historical Park
1048 Park Road #49
Stonewall, Texas 78671

There are two parks encompassed in the Lyndon B. Johnson National Historical Park: the LBJ Ranch District and the Johnson City District. The Johnson City District is the location of Johnson's Boyhood Home, and the LBJ Ranch District in Stonewall is where you will find his birthplace, the Ranch House (aka the Texas White House), and LBJ's final resting place. I suggest that you begin your visit at the LBJ Ranch District in Stonewall, Texas. Start your tours at the Lyndon B. Johnson National Historical Park Visitor Center.

Johnson City, Texas

Lyndon Baines Johnson
Childhood Home
Open to the public
Lyndon B. Johnson National Historical Park[102]
Johnson City District
National Park Service
100 East Ladybird Lane
Johnson City, Texas 78636

The Childhood Home and Johnson City District Settlement are open to the public from 9:00 a.m. to 5:00 p.m. every day except Thanksgiving, Christmas, and New Year's Day. The LBJ Ranch District in Stonewall is fourteen miles west.

The Boyhood Home is part of the Lyndon B. Johnson National Historical Park, Johnson City District. The Johnson family moved from Stonewall to Johnson City when their son Lyndon was five years old. Lyndon Johnson lived here until he was twenty-six years old. The house has been restored to reflect what life was like in the 1920s.

---

[102] https://www.nps.gov/lyjo/planyourvisit/boyhoodhome.htm

Midland, Texas

George W. Bush
Childhood Home
Open to the public
The George W. Bush Childhood Home[103]
1412 West Ohio Avenue
Midland, Texas 79701

There is a historical marker, and the childhood home is open to the public Tuesdays through Saturdays from 10:00 a.m. to 5:00 p.m. and on Sundays from 2:00 p.m. to 5:00 p.m. Tours run until 4:30 p.m. Closed on Mondays, Easter, Thanksgiving, Christmas, and New Year's Day.

This one-story, three-bedroom ranch house was built in 1939. George and Barbara Bush moved their family here in 1951, when their son George W. Bush was five years old. The house has been restored to how it was between 1951–1955. A museum, gift shop, and visitor center are housed in a nearby neighborhood home during ongoing restorations.

---

[103] http://www.bushchildhoodhome.org/

Stonewall, Texas

Lyndon Baines Johnson
Birthplace
Open to the public
Lyndon B. Johnson National Historical Park[104]
National Park Service
199 Park Road #52
Stonewall, Texas 78671

The LBJ Ranch District with the reconstructed replica of the birthplace house is open daily from 9:00 a.m. to 5:00 p.m. Closed on Thanksgiving, Christmas, and New Year's Day.

On August 27, 1908, Lyndon Baines Johnson was born in a five-room cottage built in 1889, which is where he spent his first five years. Although this house is no longer standing, you can still visit the birthplace. During his presidency, LBJ hired an architect to reconstruct the birthplace using whatever they could salvage from the original home. With the help of photos and family memories, they were able to replicate the house with authentic period pieces.

Tours begin at the LBJ State Park and Historic Site Visitor Center, where you obtain a CD and map to begin your driving tour. Your stops include the one-room schoolhouse that LBJ attended, the reconstructed birthplace, the Johnson Family Cemetery, LBJ's grandparents' farmhouse, the ranch house known as the Texas White House, and the Show Barn. Continue your tour to the Johnson City District Visitor Center, which is fourteen miles east on Route 290.

---

[104] https://www.nps.gov/lyjo/planyourvisit/reconstructedbirthplace.htm

Stonewall, Texas

Lyndon Baines Johnson
Texas White House
Open to the public
Lyndon B. Johnson National Historical Park
National Park Service
199 Park Road #52
Stonewall, Texas 78671

The LBJ Ranch District with the Johnson Family Cemetery and reconstructed birthplace is open daily from 9:00 a.m. to 5:00 p.m. Closed on Thanksgiving, Christmas, and New Year's Day.

The LBJ Ranch tells the story of the president's life. Nothing pleased Johnson more than showing off his Texas ranch. He entertained close friends as well as dignitaries from around the world. One of his favorite things to do was load guests into one of his Cadillacs with the roof down to show them around the fifteen-hundred-acre farm. He'd love to scare his guests and drive into the fields where the long-horned cattle roamed. He'd laugh as the Secret Service tried to keep up with him in the trailing cars. He preserved the property so everyone could experience his joy. With admiration, he stated, "All the world is welcome here."

Drive through the fields of buffalo and Hereford cattle that Johnson wanted to stay on the working farm for visitors to see. At the Texas White House, climb aboard the Air Force One airplane that Johnson used to fly to and from his ranch. Tour the home and learn about the life of Lyndon and Ladybird Johnson. Tours begin at the visitor center, where there are exhibits and films that depict the life of the former president. Visit the Boyhood Home, the Johnson Settlement exhibits, the Dog-trot Cabin, the Bruckner-Barn, the Windmill, the Water Tank and Cooler House, and the Withers & Spauldings General Store. The store is now a National Park Service exhibit and visitor center.

Stonewall, Texas

Lyndon Baines Johnson
Final Resting Place
Open to the public
Lyndon B. Johnson National Historical Park
National Park Service
199 Park Road #52
Stonewall, Texas 78671

The LBJ Ranch District with the Johnson Family Cemetery is open daily from 9:00 a.m. to 5:00 p.m. Closed on Thanksgiving, Christmas, and New Year's Day.

Lyndon B. Johnson died on January 22, 1973. He had already chosen his final resting place on the hillside in the family cemetery close to his birthplace home. The cemetery is part of the LBJ Ranch District in the Lyndon B. Johnson National Historical Park. Before Johnson died, he spent time walking through the cemetery, enjoying the beauty of the hillside in the shade of the old oak trees.

VERMONT

1. **Fairfield, Vermont**
   Birthplace: Chester A. Arthur

2. **Manchester, Vermont**
   Museum: Abraham Lincoln

3. **Plymouth Notch, Vermont**
   Birthplace: Calvin Coolidge
   Childhood Home: Calvin Coolidge
   Final Resting Place: Calvin Coolidge

Fairfield, Vermont

Chester A. Arthur
Birthplace
Open to the public
Chester A. Arthur Birthplace
4588 Chester Arthur Road
Fairfield, Vermont 05455

Open from June to Columbus Day on Wednesdays through Saturdays (an extremely remote area—be sure to call ahead).

Chester Alan Arthur was born on October 5, 1829, in a remote town in northern Vermont. Arthur's father, a Baptist minister, had just been transferred to the town's church, so they had moved over the border from Canada. The structure is a replica that has exhibits of Arthur's life on display. There is a marker and monument on the beautifully landscaped countryside.

This "off the beaten path" birthplace was memorable for me. I traveled to this remote area with my city-boy husband in his shiny dress shoes. We stopped at the corner kitchen for a snack, and he parked his shiny black car alongside the dusty, dented pickup trucks. We were obviously not locals, and I had to laugh at the looks we were getting. My husband is a good sport! If you go to this remote site, you really must be a dedicated follower of the presidents.

Manchester, Vermont

Abraham Lincoln
Museum
Open to the public
The Lincoln Family Home at Hildene
1005 Hildene Road
Manchester, Vermont 05255

Open daily from 9:30 a.m. to 4:30 p.m. Closed on Thanksgiving, December 24, 25, 26, and Easter.

This is a small yet very well-done museum inside the home of Lincoln's son, Robert. Hildene is a working farm with goats and cheesemaking. Tour the home of Robert and Mary Lincoln, the only son of Abe Lincoln to survive to adulthood. One of the three remaining famous hats of Lincoln, photos, and documents are on display. See Sunbeam, a 1903 Pullman car built when Robert Lincoln was president of the Pullman Company. Stroll through the gardens and acres of paths while viewing the breathtaking sights of the Vermont landscape. Shop in the Country Museum Store, where you will find many unique Vermont treasures as well as Lincoln books and collectibles.

Plymouth Notch, Vermont

Calvin Coolidge
Birthplace/Childhood Home
Open to the public
President Calvin Coolidge State Historic Site[105]
National Park Service
3780 Route 100A
Plymouth Notch, Vermont 05056

Open daily May through mid-October from 9:30 a.m. to 5:00 p.m. Start your tour at the visitor center.

Go back in time when you visit this beautiful village located in the Green Mountains of Vermont that remains almost exactly as it had been when Calvin Coolidge was born on July 4, 1872. Start your tour at the visitor center to view a short film on his life and walk through a small museum of his presidency. Then, spend the day touring the village and his birthplace cottage, which contains the original furnishings, including the bed where Coolidge was born. You can shop in the General Store and cross the street to his boyhood family home, where Coolidge was inaugurated into office by his father after the death of President Harding on August 3, 1923. Visit his church, several barns, a restaurant, and the cheese factory. Return through the visitor center, and stop in the gift shop. Don't forget to cross the street to visit the cemetery.

---

[105] https://www.nps.gov/nr/travel/presidents/calvin_coolidge_homestead.html

Plymouth Notch, Vermont

Calvin Coolidge
Final Resting Place
Open to the public
National Park Service
President Calvin Coolidge State Historic Site
3780 Route 100A
Plymouth Notch, Vermont 05056

Calvin Coolidge died on January 5, 1933. He is buried on the hillside in the family cemetery alongside many generations of the Coolidge family. The modest granite headstone is easy to find along the country road, which is across the street from the Calvin Coolidge State Historic Site.

VIRGINIA

1. **Arlington, Virginia**
   Final Resting Place: John F. Kennedy
   Final Resting Place: William Howard Taft

2. **Barboursville, Virginia**
   Birthplace: Zachary Taylor

3. **Charles City, Virginia**
   Birthplace: John Tyler
   Family Home: John Tyler
   Birthplace: William Henry Harrison

4. **Charlottesville, Virginia**
   Birthplace: Thomas Jefferson
   Family Home: Thomas Jefferson
   Final Resting Place: Thomas Jefferson
   Family Home: James Monroe

5. **Colonial Beach, Virginia**
   Birthplace: George Washington
   Birthplace: James Monroe

6. **Forest, Virginia**
   Retirement Retreat: Thomas Jefferson

7. **Fredericksburg, Virginia**
   Childhood Home: George Washington

8. **Montpelier Station, Virginia**
   Family Home: James Madison
   Final Resting Place: James Madison

9. **Mount Vernon, Virginia**
   Family Home: George Washington
   Final Resting Place: George Washington

10. **Orange, Virginia**
    Presidential Museum: James Madison

11. **Port Conway, Virginia**
    Birthplace: James Madison

12. **Richmond, Virginia**
    Final Resting Place: James Monroe
    Final Resting Place: John Tyler
    Childhood Home: Thomas Jefferson

13. **Staunton, Virginia**
    Birthplace: Thomas Woodrow Wilson
    Presidential Library and Museum: Thomas Woodrow Wilson

Arlington, Virginia

John F. Kennedy
Final Resting Place
Open to the public
Arlington National Cemetery[106]
Arlington, Virginia 22211

Open daily from 8:00 a.m. to 5:00 p.m. Start your tour at the welcome center.

John F. Kennedy was assassinated on November 22, 1963. He is buried in Arlington National Cemetery, which is across the Potomac River from our country's capital, Washington, D.C. You can start at the visitor center or take a tour bus from Washington, D.C. Kennedy's wife, Jacqueline, is also buried here. The Eternal Flame burns in the center of a flat circular five-foot granite stone.

---

[106] https://www.arlingtoncemetery.mil

Arlington, Virginia

William Howard Taft
Final Resting Place
Open to the public
Arlington National Cemetery[107]
Arlington, Virginia 22211

Open daily from 8:00 a.m. to 5:00 p.m. Start your tour at the welcome center.

William Howard Taft died on March 8, 1930. Taft's grave is easy to see, as most of the graves have small white crosses. Taft has a beautiful tall granite monument. His wife, Nellie, is also buried here. There are signs that direct you to its location. Taft and Kennedy are the only two presidents buried in Arlington National Cemetery.

---

[107] http://www.arlingtoncemetery.mil

Barboursville, Virginia

Zachary Taylor
Birthplace
Not open to the public
Montebello[108]
7350 Spotswood Trail and Old Montebello Drive
Barboursville, Virginia 22942

While traveling, Taylor's parents stayed in a cabin at their relative's house. During their stay, their son Zachary Taylor was born on November 24, 1784. Although the cabin no longer exists, there is a roadside historical sign to mark the location.

---

[108] http://www.presidentsusa.net/taylorbirthplace.html

Charles City, Virginia

John Tyler
Birthplace
Not open to the public
Greenway
10920 John Tyler Memorial Highway
Charles City, Virginia 23030

John Tyler was born on March 29, 1790. The home is now a private residence and is not open to the public. There is a historical marker in front of the home that reads:

GREENWAY
This was the home of John
Tyler, Governor of Virginia,
1808–1811. His son John Tyler,
President of the United States,
was born here, March 29, 1790.

Charles City, Virginia

John Tyler
Family Home
Open to the public
Sherwood Forest Plantation[109]
14501 John Tyler Memorial Highway
Charles City, Virginia 23030

The grounds are open daily except for Thanksgiving and Christmas. The home is open by appointment only.

Tyler purchased this house in 1842. Built in 1720, it is over three hundred feet long and is known to be the longest frame house in America, with a sixty-eight-foot ballroom. Visit the gardens and several other buildings, including the slave quarters. Tyler and his wife retired to Sherwood Forest Plantation after his presidency, and they lived here from 1842 until he died in 1862. Here, they raised seven of his fifteen children. During your visit, be sure to keep an eye out for the Gray Lady, the ghost of the house, who is said to visit from time to time.

---

[109] http://www.sherwoodforest.org/

Charles City, Virginia

William Henry Harrison
Birthplace
Open to the public
Berkeley Plantation[110]
12602 Harrison Landing Road
Charles City, Virginia 23030

The home at the Berkeley Plantation was built on the one-thousand-acre estate in 1726 by the grandfather of William Henry Harrison. The three-story brick Georgian-style mansion actually became famous for being the birthplace of Harrison's father, Benjamin Harrison V, one of the signers of the Declaration of Independence. The Berkeley Plantation's history began in 1619, when the first settlers in our country claim to have observed the first official Thanksgiving here. This plantation was also the birthplace of William Henry Harrison, the ninth president of the United States, who was born here on February 9, 1773.

House tours begin in the visitor center. Docents dressed in period clothing bring you through the home, which is furnished with eighteenth-century artifacts, and tell the story of the home from the 1600s to its importance today. In the basement, there is a small museum. After the tour, visit the gift shop and walk through the spectacular gardens along the banks of the river.

---

[110] www.berkeleyplantation.com

Charlottesville, Virginia

Thomas Jefferson
Birthplace
Not open to the public
Shadwell
Richmond Road (Route 250)
Charlottesville, Virginia 22902

On April 13, 1743, Thomas Jefferson was born on the plantation called Shadwell, named for his mother's church in England. Jefferson only lived in this home for a short time before moving. He later inherited the Shadwell plantation from his father. On February 1, 1770, the building burned to the ground. There is a roadside marker that indicates the location.

Charlottesville, Virginia

Thomas Jefferson
Family Home
Open to the public
Monticello[111]
The Thomas Jefferson Memorial Foundation
931 Thomas Jefferson Parkway
Charlottesville, Virginia 22902

Open daily from 10:00 a.m. to 5:00 p.m. Closed on Christmas. There are a variety of tours daily; check the website or ask at the visitor center.

Designed and built by Thomas Jefferson, *Monticello* is Italian for "Little Mountain." Jefferson moved into the house in 1770, married in 1772, and continued to build and rebuild for a period of over forty years. While in the home, you can see many of his unique inventions, like his own copy machine and the five-book revolving bookstand he kept on his desk, which is my favorite. View many Native American artifacts, European art, and books he collected. There are guided tours of the scenic grounds covered with flowerbeds containing a variety of flowers. Stroll along Mulberry Row at the center of the plantation. Follow the walking path of the historic location to Jefferson's fruit and vegetable gardens that are still growing today. See the slave quarters, and go through the cellar passage in the lower house, where Jefferson had a beer and wine cellar. Learn about Sally Hemings and her life as a slave at Monticello.

Begin your tour at the Welcome Pavilion, and see a film at the theater in the Griffin Discovery Room, where visitors learn about Jefferson's life with hands-on activities for children. There is a large selection of books and gifts at the museum shop, and you can relax at the café with sandwiches and drinks.

---

[111] https://www.monticello.org

Charlottesville, Virginia

Thomas Jefferson
Final Resting Place
Open to the public
Monticello
The Thomas Jefferson Memorial Foundation
931 Thomas Jefferson Parkway
Charlottesville, Virginia 22902

Thomas Jefferson died at Monticello on July 4, 1826, on the fiftieth anniversary of the signing of the Declaration of Independence and on the very same day as President John Adams. Jefferson had already designed his monument, written what he'd wanted to be inscribed on his stone, and planned where he was to be buried. While touring the grounds at Monticello, follow signs to the path that brings you to the secluded section in the woods that is Jefferson's final resting place. The family cemetery is enclosed by an iron fence to prevent vandalism but is visible to the public.

Charlottesville, Virginia

James Monroe
Family Home
Open to the public
Highland[112]
2050 James Monroe Parkway
Charlottesville, Virginia 22902

Open November through March from 11:00 a.m. to 5:00 p.m. and April through October from 9:00 a.m. to 6:00 p.m. Closed on Thanksgiving, Christmas, and New Year's Day.

The Highland Estate was purchased in 1793, but Monroe did not move in until he returned from France in 1799. Due to financial struggles, he sold the property in 1826. At that time, the new owner renamed the property Ash Lawn. In the 1920s, the property was obtained by the College of William and Mary and restored to an 1800s appearance with many of Monroe's possessions. The home is decorated with several furnishings he'd acquired while serving as minister to France. Stop in at the visitor center and gift shop, tour the homes, view the gardens and slave quarters, spend time in the boxwood gardens at the statue, and gaze at the tree believed to have been planted in Monroe's time. This estate is next to Jefferson's Monticello and can be visited on the same day if you plan an early start.

---

[112] http://highland.org/

Colonial Beach, Virginia

George Washington
Birthplace
Open to the public
George Washington Birthplace National Monument[113]
National Park Service
1732 Popes Creek Road
Colonial Beach, Virginia 22443

Open daily from 9:00 a.m. to 5:00 p.m. Closed on Thanksgiving, Christmas, and New Year's Day.

On December 25, 1779, a fire destroyed the original home where George Washington had been born on February 22, 1732. However, in 1931, a house representing a typical upper-class colonial home of the time was built on the property as a memorial. At this historic site of more than 550 acres, you can explore the grounds of the birthplace, tour the memorial house, walk the trails, picnic, then shop at the visitor center. Many sites dedicated to George Washington are always proud to say, "George Washington slept here," but here at the birthplace, they are proud to say, "George Washington slept here first."

---

[113] https://www.nps.gov/gewa/index.htm

Colonial Beach, Virginia

James Monroe
Birthplace
Open to the public
The James Monroe Birthplace[114]
4460 James Monroe Highway
Colonial Beach, Virginia 22443

Here, in 1976, the ruins of the Monroe family home were discovered by the College of William and Mary during an archaeological survey. Studies of the house foundation indicated that the family had lived in a small four-room wooden farmhouse. The James Monroe Memorial Foundation has reconstructed the home, barn, and outbuildings for the public to better understand the life of James Monroe. The grounds and visitor center are open to the public.

---

[114] https://monroefoundation.org/about-us-2/

Forest, Virginia

Thomas Jefferson
Retirement Retreat
Open to the public
Poplar Forest[115]
1542 Bateman Bridge Road
Forest, Virginia 24551

Open daily March 15 through December 30 from 10:00 a.m. to 5:00 p.m., with the last tour at 4:05 p.m. Closed on Easter, Thanksgiving, Christmas Eve, and Christmas Day.

Jefferson's dream of retirement was to distance himself from his busy home at Monticello to this faraway retreat so he could read, study, think, and spend time with family. The house embodies Jefferson's idea: his love of nature, science, and time with his grandchildren. The house was sold when Jefferson died and was destroyed by a fire in 1845. Over the last twenty years, the home has been restored to how Jefferson had designed his retreat, using his own plans and tools. Here, learn about the architecture and archeology with ongoing excavations. Visit the restoration workshop, archeology workshop, slave quarters site, reconstructed kitchen, and laundry room.

---

[115] http://www.poplarforest.org/

Fredericksburg, Virginia

George Washington
Childhood Home
Open to the public
Ferry Farm
268 Kings Highway
Fredericksburg, Virginia 22405

Open Mondays through Saturdays from 10:00 a.m. to 5:00 p.m. and on Sundays from noon to 5:00 p.m. Check the website for holiday schedules.

The family of George Washington moved to this home in 1738 when he was six years old. Start at the visitor center, which holds relics from Washington's family and artifacts from the Civil War found by archaeologists. Tour the reconstructed home decorated with replicas of 1700s furniture. Take time to explore the grounds and gardens.

Montpelier Station, Virginia

James Madison
Family Home
Open to the public
Montpelier[116]
11350 Constitution Highway
Montpelier Station, Virginia 22957

Home tours are Mondays through Sundays between 10:00 a.m. and 3:00 p.m. every half hour. The visitor center is open from 9:00 a.m. to 5:00 p.m. Check the website for other tours and hours.

Tours of Montpelier are available with many changing exhibits, including a visit to Madison's fifty-five-room home built in 1755 by his father. Explore the life of James and Dolly on the 2,600-acre estate and farm with many of the original buildings. The visitor center and museum, as well as an award-winning restaurant, are open. One interesting event is the annual Montpelier Hunt Race Day with steeplechase racing. Tickets must be purchased in advance for this popular event.

---

[116] https://www.montpelier.org

Montpelier Station, Virginia

James Madison
Final Resting Place
Open to the public
Madison Family Cemetery[117]
Montpelier Estate
11350 Constitution Highway
Montpelier Station, Virginia 22957

Open daily. Closed on Thanksgiving and Christmas.

James Madison died on June 28, 1836. James and Dolly Madison and many other family members are buried in this cemetery on the grounds of Montpelier. In 1857, a twenty-five-foot monument was placed on the grave.

---

[117] https://www.montpelier.org/visit

Mount Vernon, Virginia

George Washington
Family Home
Open to the public
Mount Vernon[118]
3200 Mount Vernon Memorial Highway
Mount Vernon, Virginia 22121

Open daily from 9:00 a.m. to 4:00 p.m.

George Washington acquired this estate when his older brother died in 1752. His father had built the house in 1735 on the banks of the Potomac River, and Washington expanded it into this twenty-one-room mansion. It has been restored to its 1770s appearance with elegant furnishings. You can tour the house and see the bed where Washington died. There are tours of the mansion and gardens, slave quarters, and the tombs where George Washington and his wife are buried. Stop at the visitor center for tour information and at the beautiful gift shop.

---

[118] http://www.mountvernon.org

Mount Vernon, Virginia

George Washington
Presidential Library
Open to the public
Fred W. Smith National Library[119]
3600 Mount Vernon Memorial Highway
Mount Vernon, Virginia 22121

Open April through October from 9:00 a.m. to 5:00 p.m. and November through March from 9:00 a.m. to 4:00 p.m.

The Washington Library holds a collection of Washington's books and manuscripts from the eighteenth century. The library is used for educational programs focusing on Washington's leadership.

---

[119] http://www.mountvernon.org/library

Mount Vernon, Virginia

George Washington
Final Resting Place
Open to the public
Mount Vernon[120]
3200 Mount Vernon Memorial Highway
Mount Vernon, Virginia 22121

After much controversy over where President Washington should be buried, the original resting place had been in the old family vault at his beloved Mount Vernon Estate. The old vault sat close to the Potomac River and was often flooded. George Washington had put in his will that a new tomb was to be constructed to replace the old family vault built in 1745. It wasn't until 1837 that the new one was completed, and the bodies of George and Martha Washington were carefully moved. The bodies were put into the tomb, each in a marble sarcophagus, that now sits in the vault behind iron gates. Viewing at this site is available.

---

[120] https://www.mountvernon.org/

Orange, Virginia

James Madison
Presidential Museum
Open to the public
James Madison Museum of Orange County Heritage[121]
129 Caroline Street
Orange, Virginia 22960

Open Tuesdays through Saturdays from 11:00 a.m. to 5:00 p.m.

This museum houses a large collection of James Madison memorabilia as well as Orange County historical exhibits, including the 1732 cube house. There are exhibits in the Black History Room and in the Madison Room, which has a collection of James and Dolly memorabilia. There are also relics of other presidents, including Madison's favorite chair, the "Campeche Chair," that was a gift from his friend Thomas Jefferson. Be sure to stop at the gift shop for books and collectibles.

---

[121] https://www.thejamesmadisonmuseum.net/

Port Conway, Virginia

James Madison
Birthplace
Open to the public
James Madison Historic Birthplace Marker
17062 James Madison Parkway (US Route 301)
King George, Virginia 22485

Madison was born on March 16, 1751, at the home of his maternal grandparents. There is a historical marker on the roadside at the Emmanuel Episcopal Church, but the home built in the 1720s no longer exists. However, you can tour the Belle Grove Plantation that was later constructed on the same property. The tour guides go into the history of the plantation during Madison's time.

Richmond, Virginia

James Monroe
Final Resting Place
Open to the public
Hollywood Cemetery[122]
412 South Cherry Street
Richmond, Virginia 23220

Open daily from 8:00 a.m. to 5:00 p.m.

James Monroe died on July 4, 1831, at his daughter's home in New York City. He was buried in Marble Cemetery in his son-in-law's family vault and was moved from New York City to Hollywood Cemetery in Richmond, Virginia, on July 5, 1858. His grave is now on a hillside in Richmond, in the unusual Gothic-style tomb known as "The Birdcage." There are walking tours through the beautifully landscaped Hollywood Cemetery. Walk through the 135 acres of gardens and paths with amazing views. Known as "the most beautiful and historic cemetery" where Presidents James Monroe and John Tyler and six Virginia governors are buried, it is also the final resting place of eighteen thousand Confederate soldiers as well as Jefferson Davis, the only president of the Confederate States of America.

[122] http://www.hollywoodcemetery.org

Richmond, Virginia

John Tyler
Final Resting Place
Open to the public
Hollywood Cemetery[123]
412 South Cherry Street
Richmond, Virginia 23220

Open daily from 8:00 a.m. to 5:00 p.m.

John Tyler died on January 18, 1862, after a short illness. He had a Confederate flag draped over his coffin and was laid to rest in Richmond, the Confederate capital. A seventeen-foot-tall granite stone marks his grave.

---

[123] http://www.hollywoodcemetery.org/

Richmond, Virginia

Thomas Jefferson
Childhood Home
Open to the public
Tuckahoe Plantation[124]
12601 River Road
Richmond, Virginia 23238

The home is open on Sundays year-round from 1:00 p.m. to 4:00 p.m. The grounds are open daily from 9:00 a.m. to sunset.

Built in the 1730s and 1740s, Tuckahoe Plantation was the childhood home of Thomas Jefferson. It was originally a twenty-five-thousand-acre tobacco and livestock plantation cared for by Jefferson's parents, Peter and Jane Jefferson. Thomas Jefferson attended school here in the one-room schoolhouse that is still standing nearby. After your house tour, take a self-guided tour of the grounds, historical buildings, and beautifully kept gardens.

---

[124] https://visithistorictuckahoe.com/

Staunton, Virginia

Thomas Woodrow Wilson
Birthplace
Open to the public
The Woodrow Wilson Presidential Library and Museum[125]
20 North Coalter Street
Staunton, Virginia 24401

Open Mondays through Saturdays from 9:00 a.m. to 5:00 p.m. and on Sundays from noon to 5:00 p.m. Closed on Thanksgiving, Christmas, and New Year's Day.

Built in 1846, this is the original home where Thomas Woodrow Wilson was born on December 28, 1856. Take a guided tour of the Presbyterian manse, where you can learn about the family and lifestyle of the 1850s. There are many original pieces, including the crib of the future president. The museum and garden tours are self-guided.

---

[125] http://www.woodrowwilson.org

Staunton, Virginia

Thomas Woodrow Wilson
Presidential Library and Museum
Open to the public
The Woodrow Wilson Presidential Library and Museum[126]
20 North Coalter Street
Staunton, Virginia 24401

Open March through December on Mondays through Saturdays from 9:00 a.m. to 5:00 p.m. and on Sundays from noon to 5:00 p.m. Closed on Thanksgiving, Christmas, and New Year's Day. During January and February, it is open Thursdays through Mondays.

This museum houses memorabilia from throughout Wilson's life before and during his presidency. Take a self-guided tour through seven galleries, and visit the WWI exhibit with weapons and uniforms. Wilson's 1919 Pierce-Arrow Limousine is also on display. The museum is part of the Birthplace Museum. Visit the museum shop for information.

---

[126] http://www.woodrowwilson.org

WASHINGTON, D.C.

1. **Washington, D.C.**
   Retreat: Abraham Lincoln
   Presidential Memorial: Thomas Woodrow Wilson
   Family Home: Thomas Woodrow Wilson
   Final Resting Place: Thomas Woodrow Wilson
   Assassination Site: Abraham Lincoln

Washington, D.C.

Abraham Lincoln
Retreat
Open to the public
President Lincoln's Cottage[127]
National Park Service
140 Rock Creek Church Road NW
Washington, D.C. 20011

The visitor center is open Mondays through Saturdays from 9:30 a.m. to 4:30 p.m., with the first tour at 10:00 a.m. and the last tour at 3:00 p.m. Closed on Thanksgiving, Christmas, and New Year's Day.

This is a slightly different home tour that focuses more on the president's life during the Civil War. Start at the visitor center on the grounds of the Armed Forces Retirement Home. There are programs and exhibits about Lincoln's experience while living here from 1862 to 1864. Storytellers bring you the president's experiences in the home they call Lincoln's Summer White House. There's art and artifacts from Lincoln's time here. It was in this cottage that President Lincoln wrote the final draft of the Emancipation Proclamation.

---

[127] www.lincolncottage.org

Washington, D.C.

Woodrow Wilson
Presidential Memorial
Open to the public
The Woodrow Wilson Presidential Memorial Exhibit at The Wilson Center[128]
Ronald Reagan Building and International Trade Center
1300 Pennsylvania Avenue NW
Washington, D.C. 20004

Open Mondays through Fridays from 9:00 a.m. to 5:00 p.m. Closed on Saturdays and Sundays.

This exhibit has interactive touch displays with information about the life of Woodrow Wilson during his presidential time. There are photos and short videos.

---

[128] https://www.wilsoncenter.org/woodrow-wilson-presidential-exhibit

Washington, D.C.

Thomas Woodrow Wilson
Family Home
Open to the public
Woodrow Wilson House
2340 South Street NW
Washington, D.C. 20008

Open March through December on Wednesdays through Sundays from 10:00 a.m. to 4:00 p.m. Closed on Mondays, Tuesdays, and holidays including Easter, Thanksgiving, and Christmas.

Learn about the life of Wilson after he left the White House. Wilson and his wife, Edith, retired to this three-story brick Georgian-Revival home. The house is full of furniture, art, artifacts, and Wilson's possessions from when he lived here in 1921 until his death in 1924. View his library and the portraits of both Wilson and Edith.

Washington, D.C.

Thomas Woodrow Wilson
Final Resting Place
Open to the public
Washington National Cathedral[129]
3101 Wisconsin Avenue NW
Washington, D.C. 20016

This church has a fourteenth-century Gothic-style design. Wilson's tomb is in the Wilson Memorial Bay in the main cathedral. There are decorated stained-glass windows, memorial statues, and beautiful flower gardens surrounding the church. Call for hours on the day you want to visit.

---

[129] http://cathedral.org/

Washington, D.C.

Abraham Lincoln
Assassination Site
Open to the public
Ford's Theater
511 Tenth Street NW
Washington, D.C. 20004

There are four exhibits to visit while at Ford's Theater. You can see rare artifacts at the museum, tour the theater with a ranger from the National Park Service, cross the street to visit the Peterson House where Lincoln died, then follow the funeral train in the Aftermath Exhibits. It is still an operating theater, so call for hours on the day you want to visit.

NATIONAL ARCHIVES'S PRESIDENTIAL LIBRARIES AND MUSEUMS

Herbert Hoover Library and Museum
Franklin D. Roosevelt Library and Museum
Harry S. Truman Library and Museum
Dwight D. Eisenhower Library and Museum
John F. Kennedy Library and Museum
Lyndon Baines Johnson Library and Museum
Richard Nixon Library and Museum
Gerald R. Ford Library and Museum
Jimmy Carter Library and Museum
Ronald Reagan Library and Museum
George Bush Library and Museum
William Clinton Library and Museum
George W. Bush Library and Museum

If you are going to visit the National Archives's Presidential Libraries and Museums, I suggest buying a membership. There are several choices for types of memberships (I bought a family one). With a membership, you will have free admission to all of the libraries and museums, as well as many other benefits.[130]

I also suggest buying a "Passport to the Presidential Libraries." Take the passport with you to each of these Presidential Libraries' admission desks or museum stores to get your book stamped. Once you have collected a stamp from each of the thirteen libraries, present it at the final museum store for a special gift.

---

[130] https://www.archivesfoundation.org/membership/

PRIVATELY OWNED PRESIDENTIAL LIBRARIES AND MUSEUMS

George Washington   Mount Vernon, Virginia
                       Morristown, New Jersey

John Adams   Quincy, Massachusetts

James Madison   Orange, Virginia

John Quincy Adams   Quincy, Massachusetts

Abraham Lincoln   Lincoln, Illinois
                       Springfield, Illinois
                       Hodgenville, Kentucky
                       Harrogate, Tennessee
                       Manchester, Vermont
                       Washington D.C.

Andrew Johnson   Greenville, Tennessee

Ulysses S. Grant   St. Louis, Missouri
                       Starkville, Mississippi

Rutherford B. Hayes   Freemont, Ohio

William McKinley   Canton, Ohio

Theodore Roosevelt   Medora, North Dakota

Woodrow Wilson   Staunton, Virginia

Warren G. Harding   Marion, Ohio

Calvin Coolidge   Northampton, Massachusetts

Ronald Reagan   Eureka, Illinois

John F. Kennedy   Hyannis, Massachusetts

Barack Obama   Chicago, Illinois

PRESIDENTIAL CHECKLIST
George Washington

Birthplace
George Washington Birthplace National Monument
National Park Service, 1732 Popes Creek Road, Colonial Beach, Virginia 22443
Notes from the visitor:

Childhood Home
George Washington Boyhood Home at Ferry Farm
268 Kings Highway, Fredericksburg, Virginia 22405
Notes from the visitor:

Headquarters Museum
Washington Headquarters Museum, Morristown National Historical Park
30 Washington Place, Morristown, New Jersey 07960
Notes from the visitor:

Headquarters Museum
George Washington Headquarters Museum Historic Site at Tappan
Livingston Street & Oak Tree Road, Tappan, New York 10983
Notes from the visitor:

Ancestral Home
Sulgrave Manor
Manor Road, Sulgrave, Banbury OX17 2SD, United Kingdom
Notes from the visitor:

Fred W. Smith National Library
Mount Vernon
3600 Mount Vernon Memorial Highway, Mount Vernon, Virginia 22121
Notes from the visitor:

Family Home
Mount Vernon
3200 Mount Vernon Memorial Highway, Mount Vernon, Virginia 22121
Notes from the visitor:

Final Resting Place
Mount Vernon
3200 Mount Vernon Memorial Highway, Mount Vernon, Virginia 22121
Notes from the visitor:

John Adams

Birthplace
John Adams Birthplace
133 Franklin Street, Quincy, Massachusetts 02169
Notes from the visitor:

Historic Park
National Park Service Visitor Center
1250 Hancock Street, Quincy, Massachusetts 02169
Notes from the visitor:

Family Home
The Old House at Peace field
135 Adams Street, Quincy, Massachusetts 02169
Notes from the visitor:

Final Resting Place
United First Parish Church
1306 Hancock Street, Quincy, Massachusetts 02169
Notes from the visitor:

Thomas Jefferson

Birthplace
Shadwell Historic Marker
Richmond Road (Route 250), Intersection Highway 64, Charlottesville, Virginia 22902
Notes from the visitor:

Childhood Home
Tuckahoe Plantation
12601 River Road, Richmond, Virginia 23238
Notes from the visitor:

Family Home
Monticello
931 Thomas Jefferson Parkway, Charlottesville, Virginia 22902
Notes from the visitor:

Retirement Home
Poplar Forest
1542 Bateman Bridge Road, Forest, Virginia 24551
Notes from the visitor:

Final Resting Place
Monticello
931 Thomas Jefferson Parkway, Charlottesville, Virginia 22902
Notes from the visitor:

James Madison

Birthplace
Historical Marker
17062 James Madison Parkway (US Route 301), King George, Virginia 22485
Notes from the visitor:

Presidential Museum
James Madison Museum of Orange County Heritage
129 Caroline Street, Orange, Virginia 22960
Notes from the visitor:

Family Home
Montpelier
11350 Constitution Highway, Montpelier Station, Virginia 22957
Notes from the visitor:

Final Resting Place
Madison Family Cemetery, Montpelier
11350 Constitution Highway, Montpelier Station, Virginia 22957
Notes from the visitor:

James Monroe

Birthplace
The James Monroe Birthplace and Visitor Center
4460 James Monroe Highway (Route 205), Colonial Beach, Virginia 22443
Notes from the visitor:

Family Home
Highland
2050 James Monroe Parkway, Charlottesville, Virginia 22902
Notes from the visitor:

Final Resting Place
Hollywood Cemetery
412 South Cherry Street, Richmond, Virginia 23220
Notes from the visitor:

John Quincy Adams

Birthplace
John Quincy Adams Birthplace
141 Franklin Street, Quincy, Massachusetts 02169
Notes from the visitor:

Historic Park
National Park Service Visitor Center
1250 Hancock Street, Quincy, Massachusetts 02169
Notes from the visitor:

Family Home
The Old House at Peace field
135 Adams Street, Quincy, Massachusetts 02169
Notes from the visitor:

Final Resting Place
United First Parish Church
1306 Hancock Street, Quincy, Massachusetts 02169
Notes from the visitor:

Andrew Jackson

Birthplace
Historical Marker
701 West South Main Street, Waxhaw, North Carolina 28173
Notes from the visitor:

Birthplace
Andrew Jackson State Park
196 Andrew Jackson Park Road, Lancaster, South Carolina 29720
Notes from the visitor:

Family Home
The Hermitage
4580 Rachel's Lane, Hermitage, Tennessee 37076
Notes from the visitor:

Final Resting Place
The Hermitage
4580 Rachel's Lane, Hermitage, Tennessee 37076
Notes from the visitor:

Martin Van Buren

Birthplace
Historical Marker, Private Residence
46 Hudson Street, Kinderhook, New York 12106
Notes from the visitor:

Family Home
National Park Service, Lindenwald, Martin Van Buren National Historic Site
1013 Old Post Road, Kinderhook, New York 12106
Notes from the visitor:

Final Resting Place
Kinderhook Village Cemetery, Kinderhook Reformed Church Cemetery
Albany Avenue and Kindertree Drive, Kinderhook, New York 12106
Notes from the visitor:

William Henry Harrison

Birthplace
Berkeley Plantation
12602 Harrison Landing Road, Charles City, Virginia 23030
Notes from the visitor:

Family Home
Grouseland, Harrison Mansion, "White House of the West"
3 West Scott Street, Vincennes, Indiana 47591
Notes from the visitor:

Final Resting Place
William Henry Harrison Tomb
41 Cliff Road, North Bend, Ohio 45052
Notes from the visitor:

John Tyler

Birthplace
Historical Marker, Private Residence
10920 John Tyler Memorial Highway (Route 5), Charles City, Virginia 23030
Notes from the visitor:

Family Home
Sherwood Forest Plantation
14501 John Tyler Memorial Highway, Charles City, Virginia 23030
Notes from the visitor:

Final Resting Place
Hollywood Cemetery
412 South Cherry Street, Richmond, Virginia 23220
Notes from the visitor:

James K. Polk

Birthplace
President James K. Polk Birthplace, North Carolina State Historic Site
12031 Lancaster Highway, Pineville, North Carolina 28134
Notes from the visitor:

Family Home
Historical Marker, Polk Place
211 7th Avenue North, Nashville, Tennessee 37219
Notes from the visitor:

Family Home
President James K. Polk, Home and Museum
301 West 7th Street, Columbia, Tennessee 38401
Notes from the visitor:

Final Resting Place
Tennessee State Capitol
600 Dr. Martin L King, Jr. Boulevard, Nashville, Tennessee 37243
Notes from the visitor:

Zachary Taylor

Birthplace
Historical Marker, Private Residence, Montebello
7350 Spotswood Trail and Old Montebello Drive, Barboursville, Virginia 22942
Notes from the visitor:

Family Home
Historical Marker, Springfield
5608 Apache Road, Louisville, Kentucky 40207
Notes from the visitor:

Historical Park
Fort Zachary Taylor Historic State Park
601 Howard England Way, Key West, Florida 33040
Notes from the visitor:

Final Resting Place
Zachary Taylor National Cemetery
4701 Brownsboro Road, Louisville, Kentucky 40207
Notes from the visitor:

Millard Fillmore

Birthplace
Millard Fillmore Birthplace, Historical Marker and Footprint
Fillmore Road, Moravia, New York 13118
Notes from the visitor:

Birthplace Replica
Millard Fillmore Birthplace, Fillmore Glen State Park
1686 NY 38, Moravia, New York 13118
Notes from the visitor:

Family Home
Millard Fillmore Home
24 Shearer Avenue, East Aurora, New York 14052
Notes from the visitor:

Final Resting Place
Forest Lawn Cemetery and Garden, National Register of Historic Places
1411 Delaware Avenue, Buffalo, New York 14209
Notes from the visitor:

Franklin Pierce

Birthplace
Lake Franklin Pierce
Off of Franklin Pierce Highway, Hillsborough, New Hampshire 03244
Notes from the visitor:

Childhood Home
Hillsborough Historical Society
301 2nd NH Turnpike, Hillsborough, New Hampshire 03244
Notes from the visitor:

Family Home
Pierce Manse
14 Horseshoe Pond Lane, Concord, New Hampshire 03301
Notes from the visitor:

Final Resting Place
Old North Cemetery
137 North State Street, Concord, New Hampshire 03301
Notes from the visitor:

James Buchanan

Birthplace
Buchanan Birthplace State Park
2831 Stony Batter Road, Mercersburg, Pennsylvania 17236
Notes from the visitor:

Birthplace Cabin
Mercersburg Academy
300 East Seminary Street, Mercersburg, Pennsylvania 17236
Notes from the visitor:

Childhood Home
Historic Marker, Buchanan Childhood Home
17 North Main Street, Mercersburg, Pennsylvania 17236
Notes from the visitor:

Family Home
Wheatland
230 North President Avenue, Lancaster, Pennsylvania 17603
Notes from the visitor:

Final Resting Place
Woodward Hill Cemetery, Buchanan Tomb
501 South Queen Street, Lancaster, Pennsylvania 17603
Notes from the visitor:

Abraham Lincoln

Birthplace
Abraham Lincoln Birthplace National Historic Park, National Park Service
2995 Lincoln Farm Road, Hodgenville, Kentucky 42748
Notes from the visitor:

Boyhood Home
Abraham Lincoln Boyhood Home at Knob Creek
7120 Bardstown Road, Hodgenville, Kentucky 42748
Notes from the visitor:

Museum
Abraham Lincoln Museum
66 Lincoln Square, Hodgenville, Kentucky 42748
Notes from the visitor:

Boyhood Home
Lincoln Boyhood National Memorial, National Park Service
3027 East South Street, Lincoln City, Indiana 47552
Notes from the visitor:

Family Home
Lincoln's New Salem
15588 History Lane, Petersburg, Illinois 62675
Notes from the visitor:

Family Home
Lincoln Home National Historic Site, National Park Service
413 South Eighth Street, Springfield, Illinois 62701
Notes from the visitor:

Presidential Museum and Library
Abraham Lincoln Presidential Library and Museum
212 North Sixth Street, Springfield, Illinois 62701
Notes from the visitor:

Final Resting Place
Lincoln's Tomb at Oak Ridge Cemetery
1441 Monument Avenue, Springfield, Illinois 62702
Notes from the visitor:

Museum
Lincoln Heritage Museum
1115 Nicholson Road, Lincoln, Illinois 62656
Notes from the visitor:

Museum
Abraham Lincoln Presidential Library and Museum
120 Mars-Debusk Parkway, Harrogate, Tennessee 37752
Notes from the visitor:

Family Home/Retreat
President Lincoln's Cottage
140 Rock Creek Church Road NW, Washington, D.C. 20011
Notes from the visitor:

Family Home/Museum
Hildene
1005 Hildene Road, Manchester, Vermont 05255
Notes from the visitor:

Assassination Site
Ford's Theater
511 Tenth Street NW, Washington, D.C. 20004
Notes from the visitor:

Andrew Johnson

Birthplace
Site of Birth Historic Marker, Mordecai Historic Park
123 Fayetteville Street, Raleigh, North Carolina 27601 Moved to 1 Mimosa Street, Raleigh, North Carolina 27604
Notes from the visitor:

Family Home
Andrew Johnson National Historic Site, National Park Service
101 North College Street, Greenville, Tennessee 37743
Notes from the visitor:

Presidential Library
Andrew Johnson Presidential Library and Museum
60 Shiloh Road, Greenville, Tennessee 37745
Notes from the visitor:

Final Resting Place
Andrew Johnson National Cemetery
121 Monument Avenue, Greenville, Tennessee 37743
Notes from the visitor:

Ulysses S. Grant

Birthplace
Grant's Birthplace State Memorial
1551 OH-232, Point Pleasant, Ohio 45153
Notes from the visitor:

Boyhood Home
Ulysses S Grant Boyhood Home
219 East Grant Avenue, Georgetown, Ohio 45121
Notes from the visitor:

Family Home
Grant Home
500 Bouthillier Street, Galena, Illinois 61036
Notes from the visitor:

Family Home
Ulysses S. Grant National Historic Site
7400 Grant Road, St. Louis, Missouri 63123
Notes from the visitor:

Family Home
Grant's Farm, Hardscrabble
10501 Gravois Road, St. Louis, Missouri 63123
Notes from the visitor:

Presidential Library
Ulysses S. Grant Presidential Library
Mississippi State University, 449 Hardy Road, Starkville, Mississippi 39759
Notes from the visitor:

Grant Cottage
Ulysses S. Grant Cottage State Historic Site
1000 Mount McGregor Road, Wilton, New York 12831
Notes from the visitor:

Homestead
U.S. Grant Ancestral Homestead
45 Dergenagh Road, Dungannon BT70 ITW, Northern Ireland, United Kingdom
Notes from the visitor:

Final Resting Place
General Grant National Memorial
West 122nd Street & Riverside Drive, New York, New York 10027
Notes from the visitor:

Rutherford B. Hayes

Birthplace
Rutherford B. Hayes Birthplace
17 East William Street, Delaware, Ohio 43015
Notes from the visitor:

Presidential Center
Rutherford B. Hayes Presidential Center, Spiegel Grove
1337 Hayes Avenue, Fremont, Ohio 43420
Notes from the visitor:

Family Home
Rutherford B. Hayes Presidential Center, Spiegel Grove
1337 Hayes Avenue, Fremont, Ohio 43420
Notes from the visitor:

Final Resting Place
Rutherford B. Hayes Presidential Center, Spiegel Grove
1337 Hayes Avenue, Fremont, Ohio 43420
Notes from the visitor:

James Garfield

Birthplace
James A. Garfield Memorial Cabin, Village of Moreland Hills
4350 S.O.M. Center Road, Moreland Hills, Ohio 44022
Notes from the visitor:

Family Home
Lawnfield, James A. Garfield National Historic Site, National Park Service
8095 Mentor Avenue, Mentor, Ohio 44060
Notes from the visitor:

Final Resting Place
Lake View Cemetery
12316 Euclid Avenue, Cleveland, Ohio 44106
Notes from the visitor:

Chester A. Arthur

Birthplace
Chester A. Arthur Birthplace
Historical Marker: VT 36 and VT 108, East Fairfield, Vermont 05448 Birthplace: 4588 Chester Arthur Road, Fairfield, Vermont 05455
Notes from the visitor:

Family Home (Private Residence)
Chester A. Arthur House, National Park Service
123 Lexington Avenue, New York, New York 10016
Notes from the visitor:

Ancestral Home
The Arthur Cottage
21A Dreen Road, Cullybackey, Ballymena BT42 1EB, County Antrim, Northern Ireland
Notes from the visitor:

Final Resting Place
Albany Rural Cemetery
Cemetery Avenue, Albany, New York 12204
Notes from the visitor:

Grover Cleveland

Birthplace
Grover Cleveland Birthplace, State Historic Site, Grover Cleveland Park
207 Bloomfield Avenue, Caldwell, New Jersey 07006
Notes from the visitor:

Family Home (Private Residence)
National Park Service, Westland
15 Hodge Road, Princeton, New Jersey 08540
Notes from the visitor:

Final Resting Place
Princeton Cemetery
29 Greenview Avenue, Princeton, New Jersey 08540
Notes from the visitor:

Benjamin Harrison

Birthplace (Private Residence)
Benjamin Harrison Birthplace Historical Marker
Symmes and Washington Streets, North Bend, Ohio 45052
Notes from the visitor:

Family Home
Benjamin Harrison House
1230 North Delaware Street, Indianapolis, Indiana 46202
Notes from the visitor:

Final Resting Place
Crown Hill Cemetery
700 West 38th Street, Indianapolis, Indiana 46208
Notes from the visitor:

William McKinley

Birthplace
The National McKinley Birthplace
36 South Main Street, Niles, Ohio 44446
Notes from the visitor:

Birthplace Museum
The National McKinley Birthplace Memorial and Museum
40 South Main Street, Niles, Ohio 44446
Notes from the visitor:

Boyhood Home
William McKinley Boyhood Home Historic Marker
202 South Main Street, Poland, Ohio 44514
Notes from the visitor:

Boyhood School
Poland Academy Historic Marker
50 College Street, Poland, Ohio 44514
Notes from the visitor:

Presidential Library
McKinley Presidential Library and Museum
800 McKinley Monument Drive NW, Canton, Ohio 44708
Notes from the visitor:

Family Home
Saxton McKinley House, National Park Service, National First Ladies' Library
331 South Market Avenue, Canton, Ohio 44702
Notes from the visitor:

Final Resting Place
William McKinley Tomb, National Park Service
800 McKinley Monument Drive NW, Canton, Ohio 44708
Notes from the visitor:

Theodore Roosevelt

Birthplace
National Park Service, Theodore Roosevelt Birthplace National Historic Site
28 East 20th Street, New York, New York 10003
Notes from the visitor:

Family Home
Sagamore Hill National Park Service
20 Sagamore Hill Road, Oyster Bay, New York 11771
Notes from the visitor:

Susan Alba

Inaugural Site
Theodore Roosevelt Inaugural National Historic Site
641 Delaware Avenue, Buffalo, New York 14202
Notes from the visitor:

Presidential Library
Theodore Roosevelt, Presidential Library Museum
Theodore Roosevelt National Park, Medora, North Dakota 58645
Notes from the visitor:

Final Resting Place
Youngs Memorial Cemetery
134 Cove Road, Oyster Bay, New York 11771
Notes from the visitor:

William Howard Taft

Birthplace
William Howard Taft National Historic Site, National Park Service
2038 Auburn Avenue, Cincinnati, Ohio 45219
Notes from the visitor:

Final Resting Place
Arlington National Cemetery
Arlington, Virginia 22211
Notes from the visitor:

Thomas Woodrow Wilson

Birthplace
The Woodrow Wilson Presidential Library and Museum
20 North Coalter Street, Staunton, Virginia 24401
Notes from the visitor:

Boyhood Home
Woodrow Wilson Boyhood Home
419 Seventh Street, Augusta, Georgia 30901
Notes from the visitor:

Childhood Home
Woodrow Wilson Family Home
1705 Hampton Street, Columbia, South Carolina 29201
Notes from the visitor:

Presidential Library
The Woodrow Wilson Presidential Library and Museum
20 North Coalter Street, Staunton, Virginia 24401
Notes from the visitor:

Family Home
Woodrow Wilson House
2340 South Street NW, Washington, D.C. 20008
Notes from the visitor:

Presidential Memorial
The Woodrow Wilson Presidential Memorial Exhibit at The Wilson Center, Ronald Reagan Building, and International Trade Center
1300 Pennsylvania Avenue NW, Washington, D.C. 20004
Notes from the visitor:

Final Resting Place
Woodrow Wilson Boyhood Home
3101 Wisconsin Avenue NW, Washington, D.C. 20016
Notes from the visitor:

Warren Harding

Birthplace
Historical Marker
6297 Ohio Route 97, Blooming Grove, Ohio 44833
Notes from the visitor:

Family Home
President Harding Home and Museum Ohio Historical Society
380 Mount Vernon Avenue, Marion, Ohio 43302
Notes from the visitor:

Final Resting Place
Harding Tomb, Warren Harding Memorial Park
966-870 Delaware Avenue, Marion, Ohio 43302
Notes from the visitor:

Calvin Coolidge

Birthplace
President Calvin Coolidge State Historic Site, National Park Service
3780 Route 100A, Plymouth Notch, Vermont 05056
Notes from the visitor:

Childhood Home
President Calvin Coolidge State Historic Site, National Park Service
3780 Route 100A, Plymouth Notch, Vermont 05056
Notes from the visitor:

Presidential Library
Calvin Coolidge Presidential Library and Museum
20 West Street, Northampton, Massachusetts 01060
Notes from the visitor:

Final Resting Place
President Calvin Coolidge State Historic Site, National Park Service
3780 Route 100A, Plymouth Notch, Vermont 05056
Notes from the visitor:

Herbert Hoover

Birthplace
Herbert Hoover Historic Site and Presidential Museum
110 Parkside Drive, West Branch, Iowa 52358
Notes from the visitor:

Childhood Home
Herbert Hoover-Minthorn House Museum
115 South River Street, Newberg, Oregon 97132
Notes from the visitor:

Presidential Library
Herbert Hoover Historic Site and Presidential Museum
210 Parkside Drive, West Branch, Iowa 52358
Notes from the visitor:

Final Resting Place
Herbert Hoover Historic Site and Presidential Museum
110 Parkside Drive, West Branch, Iowa 52358
Notes from the visitor:

Franklin D. Roosevelt

Birthplace
Home of the Franklin D. Roosevelt National Historic Site, National Park Service
4097 Albany Post Road, Hyde Park, New York 12538
Notes from the visitor:

Summer Home
Roosevelt Campobello International Park, National Park Service
459 Route 774, Welshpool, New Brunswick E5E 1A4, Canada
Notes from the visitor:

Presidential Library
Home of the Franklin D. Roosevelt National Historic Site, National Park Service
4097 Albany Post Road, Hyde Park, New York 12538
Notes from the visitor:

Little White House
Personal Retreat of Franklin D. Roosevelt
401 Little White House Road, Warm Springs, Georgia 31830
Notes from the visitor:

Final Resting Place
Home of Franklin D. Roosevelt National Historic Site, National Park Service
4097 Albany Post Road, Hyde Park, New York 12538
Notes from the visitor:

Harry S. Truman

Birthplace
Harry S. Truman Birthplace State Historic Site
1009 Truman Street, Lamar, Missouri 64759
Notes from the visitor:

Family Home
Truman Farm Home
12301 Blue Ridge Boulevard, Grandview, Missouri 64030
Notes from the visitor:

Family Home
Truman Home
219 North Delaware Street, Independence, Missouri 64050
Notes from the visitor:

Summer White House
Harry S. Truman Little White House
111 Front Street, Key West, Florida 33040
Notes from the visitor:

Presidential Library
Harry S. Truman Presidential Library and Museum
500 West U.S. Highway 24, Independence, Missouri 64050
Notes from the visitor:

Final Resting Place
Harry S. Truman Presidential Library and Museum
500 West U.S. Highway 24, Independence, Missouri 64050
Notes from the visitor:

Dwight D. Eisenhower

Birthplace
Eisenhower Birthplace and State Historic Site
609 South Lamar Avenue, Denison, Texas 75021
Notes from the visitor:

Childhood Home
Eisenhower Presidential Library, Museum, and Boyhood Home
200 Southeast Fourth Street, Abilene, Kansas 67410
Notes from the visitor:

Summer White House
Eisenhower House
1 Lincoln Drive, Newport, Rhode Island 02840
Notes from the visitor:

Presidential Library
Eisenhower Presidential Library and Museum
200 Southeast Fourth Street, Abilene, Kansas 67410
Notes from the visitor:

Retirement Home
Eisenhower National Historic Site National Park Service
1195 Baltimore Pike, Gettysburg, Pennsylvania 17325
Notes from the visitor:

Final Resting Place
Eisenhower Presidential Library and Museum
200 Southeast Fourth Street, Abilene, Kansas 67410
Notes from the visitor:

John F. Kennedy

Birthplace
John Fitzgerald Kennedy National Historic Site, National Park Service
83 Beals Street, Brookline, Massachusetts 02446
Notes from the visitor:

Ancestral Home
The Kennedy Homestead
Dunganstown, New Ross, County Wexford, Ireland
Notes from the visitor:

Church
St. Mary's Roman Catholic Church
12 William Street, Newport, Rhode Island 02840
Notes from the visitor:

Presidential Library
JFK Presidential Library
Columbia Point, 220 Morrissey Boulevard, Boston, Massachusetts 02125
Notes from the visitor:

Summer White House
Hammersmith Farm
225 Harrison Avenue, Newport, Rhode Island 02840
Notes from the visitor:

Winter White House
Kennedy Family Home
1095 North Ocean Boulevard, Palm Beach, Florida 33480
Notes from the visitor:

Museum
The Sixth Floor Museum at Dealey Plaza
411 Elm Street, Dallas, Texas 75202
Notes from the visitor:

Museum
John F. Kennedy Hyannis Museum
397 Main Street, Hyannis, Massachusetts 02601
Notes from the visitor:

Final Resting Place
Arlington National Cemetery
Arlington, VA 22211
Notes from the visitor:

Lyndon B. Johnson

Birthplace
Lyndon B. Johnson National Historic Park, National Park Service
199 Park Road #52, Stonewall, Texas 78671
Notes from the visitor:

Boyhood Home
National Historic Park, National Park Service
100 East Ladybird Lane, Johnson City, Texas 78636
Notes from the visitor:

Presidential Library
Lyndon Baines Johnson Library and Museum
University of Texas at Austin, 2313 Red River Street, Austin, Texas 78705
Notes from the visitor:

Texas White House
National Historic Park, National Park Service
199 Park Road #52, Stonewall, Texas 78671
Notes from the visitor:

Final Resting Place
National Historic Park, National Park Service
199 Park Road #52, Stonewall, Texas 78671
Notes from the visitor:

Richard Nixon

Birthplace
Richard Nixon Library and Museum
18001 Yorba Linda Boulevard, Yorba Linda, California 92886
Notes from the visitor:

Library and Museum
Richard Nixon Library and Museum
18001 Yorba Linda Boulevard, Yorba Linda, California 92886
Notes from the visitor:

Final Resting Place
Richard Nixon Library and Museum
18001 Yorba Linda Boulevard, Yorba Linda, California 92886
Notes from the visitor:

Gerald R. Ford

Birthplace
Gerald R. Ford Birthsite and Gardens
3202 Woolworth Avenue, Omaha, Nebraska 68105
Notes from the visitor:

Presidential Museum
Gerald R. Ford Presidential Museum
303 Pearl Street NW, Grand Rapids, Michigan 49504
Notes from the visitor:

Presidential Library
Gerald R. Ford Presidential Library
1000 Beal Avenue, Ann Arbor, Michigan 48109
Notes from the visitor:

Final Resting Place
Gerald R. Ford Presidential Library
303 Pearl Street NW, Grand Rapids, Michigan 49504
Notes from the visitor:

Jimmy Carter

Birthplace
Lillian G. Carter Health and Rehabilitation Nursing Center
225 Hospital Street, Plains, Georgia 31780
Notes from the visitor:

Childhood Home
National Park Service, Jimmy Carter National Historic Site
300 North Bond Street, Plains, Georgia 31780
Notes from the visitor:

Presidential Library
Jimmy Carter Presidential Library and Museum
441 John Lewis Freedom Parkway NE, Atlanta, Georgia 30307
Notes from the visitor:

Ronald Reagan

Birthplace
Ronald Reagan Birthplace and Museum
111 South Main Street, Tampico, Illinois 61283
Notes from the visitor:

Childhood Home
Ronald Reagan Childhood Home
104 Glassburn Street, Tampico, Illinois 61283
Notes from the visitor:

Childhood Home
Ronald Reagan Boyhood Home and Visitors Center
816 South Hennepin Avenue, Dixon, Illinois 61021
Notes from the visitor:

Western White House
Rancho Del Cielo, Young America's Foundation, Reagan Ranch Center Exhibit Galleries
217 State Street, Santa Barbara, California 93101
Notes from the visitor:

Presidential Museum
Ronald Reagan Museum
300 East College Avenue, Eureka, Illinois 61530
Notes from the visitor:

Presidential Library and Museum
Ronald Reagan Presidential Library and Museum
40 Presidential Drive, Simi Valley, California 93065
Notes from the visitor:

Final Resting Place
Ronald Reagan Presidential Library and Museum
40 Presidential Drive, Simi Valley, California 93065
Notes from the visitor:

George H. W. Bush

Birthplace
George H. W. Bush Birthplace
173 Adams Street, Milton, Massachusetts 02186
Notes from the visitor:

Church
Walker's Point
167 Ocean Avenue, Kennebunkport, Maine 04046
Notes from the visitor:

Family Home
Walker's Point
Ocean Avenue, Kennebunkport, Maine 04046
Notes from the visitor:

Presidential Library
George H. W. Bush Presidential Library and Museum
Texas A&M University, 1000 George Bush Drive West, College Station, Texas 77845
Notes from the visitor:

Final Resting Place
George H. W. Bush Presidential Library and Museum
Texas A&M University, 1000 George Bush Drive West, College Station, Texas 77845
Notes from the visitor:

Bill Clinton

Birthplace
Brazzel-Oakcrest Funeral Home
1001 South Main Street, Hope, Arkansas 71801
Notes from the visitor:

Childhood Home
Clinton Center and Birthplace, National Park Service
117 South Hervey Street, Hope, Arkansas 71801
Notes from the visitor:

Childhood Home
Bill Clinton Childhood Home
321 East 13th Street, Hope, Arkansas 71801
Notes from the visitor:

Childhood Home
Bill Clinton Childhood Home
1011 Park Avenue, Hot Springs, Arkansas 71901
Notes from the visitor:

Family Home
Clinton House Museum
930 West Clinton Drive, Fayetteville, Arkansas 72701
Notes from the visitor:

Presidential Library
William J. Clinton Presidential Center and Park
1200 President Clinton Avenue, Little Rock, Arkansas 72201
Notes from the visitor:

George W. Bush

Birthplace
Yale New Haven Hospital
20 York Street, New Haven, Connecticut 06511
Notes from the visitor:

Childhood Home
George W. Bush Childhood Home
37 Hillhouse Avenue, New Haven, Connecticut 06511
Notes from the visitor:

Childhood Home
The George W. Bush Childhood Home
1412 West Ohio Avenue, Midland, Texas 79701
Notes from the visitor:

Presidential Library
George W. Bush Library and Museum
2943 SMU Boulevard, Dallas, Texas 75205
Notes from the visitor:

Barack Obama

Birthplace
Kapiʻolani Medical Center for Women and Children
1319 Punahou Street, Honolulu, Hawaii 96826
Notes from the visitor:

Childhood Home
Barack Obama Childhood Home
6085 Kalanianaʻole Highway, Honolulu, Hawaii 96821
Notes from the visitor:

Family Home
Barack Obama Family Home
5046 South Greenwood Avenue, Chicago, Illinois 60615
Notes from the visitor:

Presidential Library
Barack Obama Center
Jackson Park, Chicago, Illinois 60615
Notes from the visitor:

Susan Alba

Donald Trump

Birthplace
Jamaica Hospital Medical Center
8900 Van Wyck Expressway, Richmond Hill, Queens, New York 11418
Notes from the visitor:

Winter White House
Mar-A-Lago
1100 South Ocean Boulevard, Palm Beach, Florida 33415
Notes from the visitor:

Family Home
Trump Towers
725 Fifth Avenue, New York, New York 10022
Notes from the visitor:

Joseph Biden

Birthplace
St. Mary's Hospital, now Yeshiva Beth Moshe School
930 Hickory Street, Scranton, Pennsylvania 18505
Notes from the visitor:

Childhood Home
Joseph Biden Childhood Home
2446 North Washington Avenue, Scranton, Pennsylvania 18509
Notes from the visitor:

Summer White House
Joseph Biden Summer White House
Rehoboth Beach, Delaware 19971
Notes from the visitor:

Family Home
Joseph Biden Family Home
1209 Barley Mill Road, Wilmington, Delaware 19807
Notes from the visitor:

ABOUT THE AUTHOR

Susan Alba is a retired elementary school teacher who lives in Providence, Rhode Island. She loved teaching her students about the history of our great country and the lives of former presidents. She also has a master's degree from Roger Williams University as a reading specialist, where she concentrated in historical fiction, a field of study that led to her passion for presidential studies. Now, she travels with her husband, Guy, and they intend to experience the history of every state in the country. Susan always has her next trip planned!

Made in the USA
Middletown, DE
18 June 2024

55977323R00246